Virginia Real Estate: Practice & Law

FIFTH EDITION

**Real Estate
Education Company**®
A Kaplan Professional Company

Vice President: Carol L. Luitjens
Executive Editor: Diana Faulhaber
Development Editor: Jerry Schwartz
Associate Real Estate Writer: Nikki Loosemore
Managing Editor: Ron Liszkowski

© 1978, 1989, 1995, 1996, 1999 by Dearborn Financial Publishing, Inc.®

Published by Real Estate Education Company®,
a division of Dearborn Financial Publishing, Inc.®,
a Kaplan Professional Company
155 North Wacker Drive
Chicago, Illinois 60606-1719
(312) 836-4400
http:\\www.dearborn.com

Printed in the United States of America.

00 01 10 9 8 7 6 5 4 3

Library of Congress Cataloging-in-Publication Data

Virginia real estate : practice & law : final draft. — 5th ed.
   p.   cm.
  Includes index.
  ISBN 0-7931-3220-7
  1. Vendors and purchasers—Virginia. 2. Real property—Virginia.
I. Real Estate Education Company.
KFV2526.Z9V57   1999
346.75504'3—dc21
                           99-20564
                           CIP

Contents

Preface

Virginia Real Estate: Practice & Law

Virginia Real Estate: Practice & Law is a key component of Real Estate Education Company®'s TOTAL LEARNING SYSTEM™. This system offers students and educators a complete turnkey package for prelicense real estate courses, continuing education and professional enrichment. As the demographics and structure of the real estate industry change, Real Estate Education Company® is helping students, instructors and practitioners adapt to this new environment by providing more accessible and versatile educational tools.

This book can be used with equal effectiveness with *any* of our principles products:

- ☐ *Modern Real Estate Practice*
- ☐ *Real Estate Fundamentals*
- ☐ *Mastering Real Estate Principles*
- ☐ *SuccessMaster™ Software — National*

Virginia Real Estate also offers current real estate professionals a practical handbook of Virginia's real estate law and rules, along with the most current developments. Every effort has been made to ensure that the information contained in this book is both relevant and current. There are also numerous references to Virginia statutes and the Real Estate Board's Rules and Regulations so readers can look up the law themselves in most public and university libraries.

Readers using *Virginia Real Estate: Practice & Law* to prepare for the state real estate licensing examination should note that this book does not address the national topics that comprise most of the real estate examination. Students are advised to first read the relevant material in one of the main principles products, then turn to *Virginia Real Estate* for a focus on Virginia's laws and practices as they relate to that subject. *This book is designed to discuss the statutes, rules and practical real estate issues that arise in the state of Virginia.*

How To Use This Book

The **Conversion Table** on the next page provides an easy reference for using this book to supplement various others. For instance, *Virginia Real Estate*'s Chapter 5, Legal Descriptions, may be read in conjunction with Chapter 9 in *Modern Real Estate Practice;* Chapter 1 in *Real Estate Fundamentals*; and Chapter 6 in both *Mastering Real Estate Principles* and *SuccessMaster, National Edition.* The chart also refers students to the *Guide to Passing the PSI Real Estate Exam.*

□ CHAPTER CONVERSION TABLE □

Virginia Real Estate: Practice & Law	Modern Real Estate Practice	Real Estate Fundamentals	Mastering Real Estate Principles	SuccessMaster Software, National Edition	Guide to Passing the PSI Real Estate Exam
1 Real Estate Brokerage & Agency	4, 5	8	13	13	5, 12
2 Listing Agreements & Buyer Representation	6	6	15	15	6
3 Interests in Real Estate	7	2	7	7	4
4 Forms of Real Estate Ownership	8	4	9	9	4
5 Legal Descriptions	9	1	6	6	4
6 Real Estate Taxes & Other Liens	10	9	5, 25	5, 26	7
7 Real Estate Contracts	11	6	14	14	6
8 Transfer of Title	12	3	10	10	4
9 Title Records	13	5	11	11	4
10 Real Estate License Laws	—	—	16	16	—
11 Real Estate Financing	14, 15	11	UNIT 7	UNIT 7	9, 10
12 Leases	16	7	8	8	6
13 Fair Housing & Ethical Practices	20	14	17	17	7

Features of This Edition

In addition to its expanded usefulness, this edition includes

- expanded coverage of Virginia **agency** issues;

- discussion of the **most current developments** in Virginia real estate laws, rules and practices;

- **end-of-chapter questions** that rigorously test students' comprehension and provide effective **exam practice;**

- an end-of-book **answer key** that includes page references for more effective learning;

- a new 40-question **practice exam** that prepares students for the Virginia portion of the licensing exam; and

- thoroughly revised text with a more **reader-friendly** and accessible style that makes the information clear and understandable without sacrificing accuracy.

Editorial Review Board

The publisher would like to thank the following people for their invaluable assistance in preparing this new edition of *Virginia Real Estate: Practice & Law.* Whether by suggesting changes to the previous edition or by reviewing the manuscript for this book, these individuals provided vital professional guidance and real-world expertise from which everyone benefits.

Donna V. Austin
Richmond Association of REALTORS⁽ᴿ⁾

Doris S. Barrell
Northern Virginia Association of REALTORS⁽ᴿ⁾

Helen R. Chapman
Colquitt Carruthers

Mary M. Otis
Northern Virginia Association of REALTORS⁽ᴿ⁾

Jim Raleigh
Hampton Roads School of Real Estate

Joseph L. Sanders
Alpha College of Real Estate

Special thanks to the **Northern Virginia Association of REALTORS®** and its members for providing the forms included in this book. The forms are included as illustrations only and may not be reproduced without the written permission of the copyright holder.

1 Real Estate Brokerage and Agency

BROKERAGE DEFINITIONS

In Virginia, a real estate *broker* is defined by statute as

> any person or business entity, including, but not limited to, a partnership, association, corporation, or limited liability corporation, who, for compensation or valuable consideration (i) sells or offers for sale, buys or offers to buy, or negotiates the purchase or sale or exchange of real estate, including units or interest in condominiums, cooperative interest . . . or time shares in a time-share program . . . or (ii) who leases or offers to lease, or rents or offers for rent, any real estate or the improvements thereon for others. [§54.1-2100]

The word *broker* refers either to a firm or sole proprietor who transacts real estate business.

The statutory definition of a real estate *salesperson* is

> . . . any person, or business entity of not more than two persons unless related by blood or marriage, who for compensation or valuable consideration is employed either directly or indirectly by, or affiliated as an independent contractor with, a real estate broker [to assist in a broker's functions]. [§54.1-2101]

A salesperson may perform the same functions as a broker. The difference is that the salesperson *must* be employed by or affiliated with a licensed real estate broker. Salespersons are considered to be general agents of the brokers they represent.

Brokers and salespersons can be defined even further, according to specific duties:

Principal Broker — the individual designated by the firm to be responsible for the real estate activities of the firm and all its licensees, and to receive correspondence from the Real Estate Board (REB).

Supervising Broker (or, *managing broker*) — an individual who holds a broker's license and who has been designated by the firm to supervise the activities of a branch office.

Associate Broker — any individual, other than the designated principal broker, who holds a broker's license. Supervising brokers are associate brokers. An associate broker usually works for a real estate broker or firm as a sales associate.

Sole Proprietor — an individual (not a corporation) who is doing business either under his or her own name, or under a legally registered fictitious name, and is fulfilling all the duties and functions of the principal broker in the firm. A sole proprietor could be a licensed broker or an unlicensed individual. A proprietor who is *not* licensed must hire a licensed broker to assume the duties of a principal broker.

Designated Agent (or *designated representative*) — a licensee designated by a broker to represent only one party to a transaction when the broker is also representing other parties in the same transaction.

Dual Agent (or *dual representative*) — a licensee (or licensees) who has a brokerage relationship within the same firm with both seller and buyer, or both landlord and tenant, in the same real estate transaction.

Common Source Information Company — any person or entity that compiles or provides information regarding real estate for sale or lease and other data, such as a multiple listing service (MLS).

WHO MUST HAVE A LICENSE

Any person or organization who performs or advertises brokerage services must be licensed by the Virginia Real Estate Board. Licenses are issued for individuals, partnerships, limited liability companies, associations and corporations and non-broker-owned sole proprietorships. Individual licenses are issued to principal brokers, associate brokers, and salespersons (*see* Chapter 10 for licensing requirements).

EXEMPTIONS

Not everyone who performs an act of real estate brokerage or related real estate activities is required to hold a Virginia real estate license. The following persons are *exempt* from the state licensing requirement:

- Individuals who are *selling or renting their own property*

- Persons selling or renting property *owned by their employers*

- Attorneys involved in real estate transactions *in their normal role as attorneys*

These and other exemptions are detailed in Chapter 10.

AGENCY

The concept of common law agency no longer exists in Virginia. In 1995, the Virginia General Assembly expressly abolished the common law

of agency in real estate transactions. [§54.1-2144]. In its place, the legislature enacted an agency statute that codifies the agency relationships among brokers, buyers, sellers, landlords and tenants. [§§54.1-2130 through 54.1-2144] This is referred to as "standard" or statutory agency.

In addition to establishing new rules and standards for agency relationships in real estate transactions, the statute provides that compensation does not create a brokerage relationship, nor does the use of a common source information company, such as an MLS. [§§54.1-2140; 54.1-2141]

Definitions

Virginia's agency statute defines the term *agency* as

> every relationship in which a real estate licensee acts for or represents a person by such person's express authority in a real estate transaction . . . [§54.1-2130]

The parties are, however, free to enter into a written agreement that establishes some other sort of relationship — for instance, where the broker is an *independent contractor*, or where additional duties are imposed on the broker. In that case, the written agreement governs the relationship, not the statute. [§54.1-2130] The lack of a specific written agreement would impose the duties of a standard agency.

A *brokerage relationship* is a contractual relationship between a client and licensee, in which the licensee has been engaged by the client to procure a seller, buyer, option, tenant or landlord, who is ready, willing and able to sell, buy, option, exchange or rent real estate. [§54.1-2130]

Note that the relationship is limited to a *client* and a broker: a client is a person who has entered into a brokerage relationship with a licensee; any other person for whom the licensee performs routine services (referred to as "ministerial acts") is a *customer*. [§54.1-2130]

Ministerial acts are routine acts that a licensee can perform for a person which do not involve discretion or the exercise of the licensee's own judgment. [§54.1-2130]

Seller's Agent: Duties to Seller

The Virginia agency statute establishes certain duties for a licensee who is in an agency relationship with a seller. [§54.1-2131A] In addition to performing under the terms of the brokerage relationship, the licensee is expected to

- *seek a sale at the price and terms established in the brokerage relationship*, or at some other price and terms acceptable to the seller (however, once the property is under contract, the licensee is not expected to continue to pursue additional offers unless he or she is required to do so under the brokerage agreement or sales contract);

- *present all written offers and counteroffers* in a timely manner, even after the property is under contract;

- *disclose* to the seller all material facts, of which the licensee has actual knowledge, related to the property or concerning the transaction;

- *account* in a timely manner for all money and property received in which the seller has or may have an interest;

- maintain *confidentiality* of all personal and financial information received from the client during the brokerage relationship, and all information characterized as confidential by the client, unless the seller consents in writing to its release or unless

the licensee is required by law to release the information;

- exercise *ordinary care*; and

- *comply with all applicable laws*, including the fair housing statutes and regulations.

The traditional agency duties of care, obedience, accounting, loyalty and disclosure (COALD) are included in the statutory scheme. Care, accounting and disclosure are expressly included; obedience and loyalty are implied by the requirement that licensees perform under the terms of the agreement with the client and maintain confidentiality. The statutory duties, however, may not be as rigorous as traditional fiduciary duties. This discrepancy arises because of the difference in fiduciary relationships which were present in the old common law of agency (positions requiring a *special* relationship of trust, confidence, or responsibility in carrying out obligations to others) and the exercise of *ordinary* care which replaces the term *fiduciary* in the new statutory law.

Seller's Agent: Duties to Buyer

Licensees who are engaged by sellers are required by statute to disclose their seller-agency relationship to the prospective buyers and treat them honestly. Prospective buyers may not knowingly be given false information. In addition, they must be informed of any material adverse facts regarding the property's physical condition of which the licensee has actual knowledge.

However, if a licensee provides false information to the prospective buyer, the licensee will not be held liable if the following conditions are met:

1. The false information was provided to the licensee by the seller; and

2. The licensee did not actually know that the information was false; *or*

3. The licensee did not act in reckless disregard of the truth. [§54.-2131B]

A licensee engaged by a seller is permitted to assist buyers and potential buyers by performing ministerial acts. The performance of ministerial acts for a buyer does not violate the licensee's brokerage relationship with the seller unless the brokerage agreement expressly prohibits such services. [§54.1-2131C] Similarly, the brokerage relationship is not violated if the licensee shows alternative properties to prospective buyers as clients or customers, or represents other sellers. [§54.1-2131D]

Buyer's Agent: Duties to Buyer

When a licensee enters into an agency relationship with a buyer, he or she has specific statutory obligations in addition to performing under the terms of the brokerage agreement. [§54.1-2132] The licensee must promote the buyer's interests by

- seeking a property at a price and under terms acceptable to the buyer;

- presenting all written offers or counteroffers in a timely manner;

- *disclosing* to the buyer all material facts, of which the licensee has actual knowledge, related to the property or concerning the transaction;

- accounting in a timely manner for all money and property received in which the buyer has an interest;

- maintaining confidentiality of all personal and financial information received from the client, as well as of all other information the client may ask be kept confiden-

tial (unless the buyer consents in writing to the information's release, or the licensee is required by law to release it);

- exercising *ordinary* care; and

- complying with all laws, including fair housing statutes and regulations.

Buyer's Agent: Duties to Sellers

Licensees who are engaged by buyers are required by statute to disclose their buyer-agency relationship to sellers and treat them honestly. Sellers may not knowingly be given false information. In the case of a residential transaction, a licensee must disclose to the seller the buyer's *intent to occupy* the property as a principal residence. [§54.1-2132B]

A buyer's agent is not prohibited from providing certain ministerial assistance to sellers, unless the brokerage agreement expressly prohibits him or her from doing so. [§54.1-2132C]

A buyer's agent may show the same properties to other prospective buyers, whether as clients or customers, without breaching any duty or obligation to the buyer. Similarly, the buyer's agent may represent multiple buyers who are looking at the same or different properties. The buyer's agent may also represent sellers of other properties. [§54.1-2132D]

Representation of Landlords and Tenants

The same obligations, duties and expectations that apply to licensees in brokerage relationships with sellers and buyers of real estate apply to licensees in similar relationships with landlords or tenants. The landlord/client or tenant/client is owed the same duties as a seller/client or buyer/client. Ministerial acts are permitted on behalf of landlord or tenant customers, and multiple landlord or tenant clients are allowed.

[§§54.1-2133; 2134] The relationship between the licensee and either the landlord or the tenant must be disclosed to all parties, as discussed below.

Property Management

Licensees who are engaged to manage real estate are required by Virginia law to exercise ordinary care; disclose all material facts; maintain confidentiality of information; account for all money and property received; and comply with all relevant real estate and fair housing laws and regulations. The licensee is expected to perform his or her services in accordance with the property management agreement. Licensees are permitted to represent other owners in the management of real property and to represent the owner as seller or landlord under a brokerage agreement. [§54.1-2135]

Establishing the Brokerage Relationship

Under Virginia's agency statute, the brokerage relationship begins at the time a client engages a licensee. [§54.1-2137A] Prior to entering into the relationship, the licensee is required to advise the prospective client:

- of the type of brokerage relationship proposed by the broker;

- of the broker's compensation; and

- whether the broker will share the compensation with a broker who may have a brokerage relationship with another party to the transaction. [§54.1-2136]

Remember, compensation does not imply or create a brokerage relationship.

Termination of Brokerage Relationship

A brokerage relationship terminates when the brokerage agreement's terms have been completely performed. However, the relationship may also be terminated by

- the expiration of the agreement;

- a mutual agreement to terminate;

- a default by any party; or

- the licensee's withdrawal when a client refuses to consent to disclosed dual agency. [§§54.1-2137A; 54.1-2139D]

All brokerage relationships must have a definite termination date. [§54.1-2137B] If an agreement lacks a definite termination date, the statute establishes a mandatory termination date of 90 days after the commencement of the brokerage relationship. [§54.1-2137B]

Once a brokerage relationship has terminated or expired, the licensee owes no further duties to the client. However, the licensee is nonetheless required to account for all monies and property and to *preserve the confidentiality* of information.

Disclosure Requirements

Certain disclosure requirements apply to sale and rental transactions. [§§54.1-2138A, B] At the time of the first substantive discussion about a specific property with an actual or prospective buyer, seller, landlord or tenant who is not a client of the licensee and who is not represented by another licensee, a licensee is required to disclose any broker relationship he or she has with any other party to the transaction. The disclosure must be made no later than the time when specific real estate assistance is first provided, and in writing at the earliest practical time for sales transactions and at the time of the application or lease, whichever is first, for rental transactions. The written disclosure must be in substantially the same form as that illustrated in Figure 1.1.

Any required disclosures may be given in combination with other disclosures or information, but if so, the disclosure must be conspicuous, printed in bold lettering, all capitals, underlined, or within a separate box. [§54.1-2139B] If the licensee's relationship with any party to the transaction changes, all clients and customers involved in the transaction must be informed of the change in writing. Copies of all disclosures must be kept for three years.

Disclosure is not required when the prospective buyer, seller, landlord or tenant is already represented by another licensee; nor is disclosure required to landlords or tenants in single- or multi-family residential units for terms of less than two months. [§54.1-2138B]

Disclosed Dual Representation

In Virginia, a licensee may represent both parties in the same real estate transaction — seller and buyer or landlord and tenant — only with the written consent of all clients in the transaction. [§54.1-2139] The client's signature on the written disclosure form is presumptive evidence of the brokerage relationship. The disclosure must be substantially in the same form as the illustration in Figure 1.2.

A dual representative does not terminate any brokerage relationship by making the required disclosures of dual representation. [§54.1-2139C] As mentioned previously, a licensee may withdraw from representing a client who refuses to consent to disclosed dual agency. The licensee may withdraw under such circumstances without liability, and may continue to represent the other client. Further, the licensee may continue to represent the client who refused dual representation in other transactions. [§54.1-2139D]

Designated Representation

A principal or supervising broker may assign different affiliated licensees as *designated representatives* to represent different clients in the same transaction. [§54.1-2139E] The appointment of designated representatives excludes other licensees in the firm from involvement in the transaction. *The use of designated representatives does not constitute dual representation if each designee represents only one client in a particular real estate transaction.* [§54.1-2139E] However, the principal or broker who is supervising the transaction is construed by law to be a dual representative. The disclosure must be made in writing, and similar to Figure 1.3.

Figure 1.1   **Disclosure of Brokerage Relationship [§54.1-2138A]**

DISCLOSURE OF BROKERAGE RELATIONSHIP

The undersigned do hereby acknowledge disclosure that:

The licensee _____
Name of Firm

represents the following party in a real estate transaction:

_____ Seller(s)   *or*   _____Buyer(s)

_____Landlord(s)   *or*   _____Tenant(s)

_____	_____
Date	*Name*
_____	_____
Date	*Name*

Figure 1.2 Disclosure of Dual Representation

DISCLOSURE OF DUAL REPRESENTATION

The undersigned do hereby acknowledge disclosure that:

The licensee(s) _____

Name of Broker, Firm or Salesperson(s)

represents more than one party in this real estate transaction as indicated below:

_____Seller(s) and Buyer(s)   _____Landlord(s) and Tenant(s)

The undersigned understands that the foregoing dual representative(s) may not disclose to either client or such client's designated representative any information that has been given to the dual representative by the other client within the confidence and trust of the brokerage relationship except for that information which is otherwise required or permitted by Article 3 (§54.1-2130 et seq.) of Chapter 21 of Title 54.1 of the Code of Virginia to be disclosed. The undersigned by signing this notice do hereby acknowledge their informed consent to the disclosed dual representation by the licensee.

_____	_____
Date	*Name (One Party)*
_____	_____
Date	*Name (One Party)*
_____	_____
Date	*Name (Other Party)*
_____	_____
Date	*Name (Other Party)*

Figure 1.3   Disclosure of the Use of Designated Representatives

---

DISCLOSURE OF THE USE OF DESIGNATED REPRESENTATIVES

The undersigned do hereby acknowledge disclosure that:

The licensee _____
                              Name of Broker and Firm

represents more than one party in this real estate transaction as indicated below:

_____ Seller(s) and Buyer(s)   _____ Landlord(s) and Tenant(s)

The undersigned understands that the foregoing dual representative may not disclose to either client or such client's designated representative any information that has been given to the dual representative by the other client within the confidence and trust of the brokerage relationship except for that information which is otherwise required or permitted by Article 3 (§54.1-2130 et seq.) of Chapter 21 of Title 54.1 of the Code of Virginia to be disclosed. The undersigned by signing this notice do hereby acknowledge their informed consent to the disclosed dual representation by the licensee.

The principal or supervising broker has assigned _____
                                                        Licensee/Sales Associate

to act as Designated Representative for the one party as indicated below:

_____ Seller(s)   *or*   _____ Buyer(s)

_____ Landlord(s)   *or*   _____ Tenant(s)

and _____ to act as Designated Representative for
        Licensee/Sales Associate

the other party as indicated below:

_____ Seller(s)   *or*   _____ Buyer(s)

_____ Landlord(s)   *or*   _____ Tenant(s)

_____   _____
      Date   *Name (One Party)*

_____   _____
      Date   *Name (One Party)*

_____   _____
      Date   *Name (Other Party)*

_____   _____
      Date   *Name (Other Party)*

Questions

1. An individual wants to sell her own house. Which of the following statements is true?

    a. She does not need a real estate license to sell her house herself.
    b. In Virginia, anyone who sells real property must have a real estate license issued by the Real Estate Board.
    c. The individual may obtain a temporary real estate license in order to legally sell her house.
    d. She may sell her house without obtaining a real estate license only if she is a licensed attorney.

2. *P* is a real estate licensee who has signed a brokerage agreement with *H*, who is looking for an apartment to rent. *P* does not charge a fee to prospective tenants; rather, *P* receives a commission from landlords. *P* tells a landlord that *H* could probably pay a somewhat higher rent than the landlord is asking. Which of the following statements is true?

    a. *P* owes the statutory agency duties to the landlords who pay the commission.
    b. *P*'s disclosure to the landlord was appropriate under these circumstances.
    c. *P*'s disclosure violated the statutory duties owed to *H*.
    d. Because *P* is not charging a fee to prospective tenants, *P* has violated Virginia's agency statute.

3. Routine services that do not create an agency relationship are referred to as

    a. transactional acts.
    b. routine brokerage.
    c. ministerial acts.
    d. customer service.

4. Any individual holding a broker's license in Virginia who is not a principal broker is a(n)

    a. affiliate broker.
    b. supervising broker.
    c. managing broker.
    d. associate broker.

5. *J* and *T* are licensed real estate salespersons who are both affiliated with FGH Realty. *J* has listed a house, and *T* has a likely buyer. What should the supervising broker do?

    a. Nothing, because neither *J* nor *T* wish to act as disclosed dual representatives, there is no legal issue.
    b. The broker's only legal option is to insist that either *J* or *T* sign a disclosed dual representation agreement with the prospective buyer and the sellers.
    c. The broker may assign *J* and *T* as designated representatives, and provide a disclosure form to the sellers only. The broker will be a subagent.
    d. The broker may assign *J* and *T* as designated representatives, and provide a disclosure form to both the sellers and the prospective buyers. The broker will be a dual agent.

LISTING AGREEMENTS

The standard types of listings — open, exclusive-agency and exclusive-right-to-sell — are all used in Virginia. Both exclusive-agency and exclusive-right-to-sell listings must have a definite termination date. The owner must be furnished a copy of the listing at the time it is signed.

Virginia Real Estate Board (REB) regulations specifically prohibit net listings [135-20-280(5)]. A *net listing* is an agreement in which an owner specifies a particular dollar amount that he or she must "net" from the sale or rental of a property; the broker may keep any amount over the seller's net that is generated by the transaction. Under a net listing, it is difficult to balance the broker's responsibility to the principal with the broker's own interest in making a profit. Because this practice is not permitted in Virginia, brokers must inform prospective clients that their fee will be a percentage of the selling price (a *commission*), or a flat fee for services.

FOR EXAMPLE . . .

O, a homeowner, called D, a Richmond real estate broker, and told her that he wanted to sell his house.

"I don't have time to be bothered with percentages and bargaining and offers and counteroffers," O explained. "I just need to walk out of this deal with $150,000 in my pocket. You sell this place for more than that, and you can keep the rest."

D knew that homes such as O's were selling for well over $200,000. On the other hand, D knew that net listings are illegal in Virginia. What should D do?

LISTING FORMS

There is no "standard" listing form used throughout the state of Virginia. Rather, local associations develop their own blank forms for the use of their members (see Figure 2.1).

IN PRACTICE . . .
In a listing form, the blanks are rarely optional. *All blanks should be filled in.* If an item does not apply in a particular transaction, the notation "N/A" ("not applicable") should be used. Finding accurate information for each item may require additional research.

Some items on the listing forms may have to be entered as approximations, such as mortgage balance (until a payoff statement is available from the lender) or age of the dwelling. Accurate figures should be used wherever possible. Any changes involving financial responsibility on the seller's part (such as a change in price) must be authorized in writing by the seller.

The following is a line-by-line analysis of the content of Figure 2.1:

Item 1: Selling price should be clearly written. Be careful not to confuse numbers. Commas and decimals points should be properly placed.

Each possible item requires a yes or no response. There is also space in which to list any other items that are not preprinted on the form. A frequent issue of disagreement between buyers and sellers involves which items convey with the property; by being clear about all possible items, licensees can avoid arguments later.

Item 2: Virginia's agency law (discussed in Chapter 1) requires a full disclosure of agency options and issues. Licensees must be certain that their client clearly understands this important information.

Item 3: Virginia law requires that all listing agreements have a definite expiration date. Such words as "ninety days from the date of this agreement" are not sufficiently definite. Failing to include a definite termination date is an act of improper dealing in violation of the rules and regulations.

Item 4: This statement of the Fair Housing law puts the seller on notice that the licensee will show the property to any qualified buyer.

Item 5: The broker may use a multiple-listing service (MLS) and related electronic databases and may distribute information about the property in print and electronic form during and after the expiration of the agreement. The seller's permission must be obtained for the broker to disclose the contract price of the property in an MLS prior to closing.

Item 6: Broker's compensation must be clearly stated, for the broker's protection as well as for the seller's information.

Item 7: This statement makes clear that there are no antitrust violations involved in the transaction.

Item 8: The owner is put on notice that there will be people entering the property. The broker disavows responsibility for loss except in the case of malfeasance on the part of a particular party — for instance, if a licensee permitted a known thief to look around the seller's home unescorted, and the seller's personal property was stolen.

Item 9: The seller is obliged to permit his or her property to be shown, inspected and appraised during reasonable hours; to cooperate with the broker; and to sign an enforceable sales contract.

Item 10: In addition to the seller's duty to cooperate, he or she retains responsibility for maintaining the property during the term of the agreement.

Item 11: Additional seller disclosures are required if the property is a cooperative or condominium.

Item 12: If the property is located in a development subject to Property Owners' Association Act, a special disclosure packet must be obtained by the seller and presented to the buyer.

Item 13: Sellers must comply with the Residential Property Disclosure Act unless they are exempt.

Item 14: If a property was built before 1978, required disclosures must be made regarding lead-based paint hazards.

Item 15: The broker must obtain the seller's permission to place a "For Sale" sign on the property and install a lockbox.

Item 16: If the property may be sold subject to an existing mortgage or deed of trust, the amount of the unpaid balance must be disclosed.

Item 17 addresses seller financing.

Item 18: If the seller is an active or inactive real estate licensee, this information must be disclosed.

Item 19: The owner or broker may add any other terms, conditions or contingencies under which the property will be sold.

Figure 2.1 Listing Agreement — Exclusive Right to Sell

VIRGINIA LISTING AGREEMENT - EXCLUSIVE RIGHT TO SELL

This Agreement is made on _____, 19 ____, by and between _____

_____ ("Seller")

and _____ ("Broker")
(Firm Name)

in consideration of providing the services and facilities described herein, the Broker is hereby granted the exclusive right to sell the Property known as:

_____, Virginia _____ ("Property").

Legal Description _____ Tax Map No. _____.

1. The Sales Price includes the following personal property and fixtures: A. Any existing built-in heating and central air conditioning equipment, plumbing and lighting fixtures, sump pump, attic fans, storm windows, storm doors, screens, installed wall-to-wall carpeting, window shades, blinds, smoke and heat detectors, tv antennas, exterior trees and shrubs and B. The items marked YES below as currently installed or offered.

YES NO ITEM	YES NO ITEM	YES NO ITEM	YES NO ITEM
❑ ❑ Stove or Range	❑ ❑ Disposer	❑ ❑ Ceiling Fan(s) # ____	❑ ❑ Alarm System
❑ ❑ Cooktop	❑ ❑ Freezer	❑ ❑ Washer	❑ ❑ Intercom
❑ ❑ Wall Oven(s) # ____	❑ ❑ Window Fan(s) # ____	❑ ❑ Dryer	❑ ❑ Storage Shed(s) # ____
❑ ❑ Refrigerator(s) # ____	❑ ❑ Window A/C Unit(s) # ____	❑ ❑ Furnace Humidifier	❑ ❑ Garage Opener(s) # ___
❑ ❑ w/ ice maker	❑ ❑ Pool, Equip. & Cover	❑ ❑ Electronic Air Filter	❑ ❑ w/ remote(s) # ___
❑ ❑ Dishwasher	❑ ❑ Hot Tub, Equip. & Cover	❑ ❑ Central Vacuum	❑ ❑ Playground Equipment
❑ ❑ Built-in Microwave	❑ ❑ Satellite Dish and Equip.	❑ ❑ Water Treatment System	❑ ❑ Wood Stove
❑ ❑ Trash Compactor	❑ ❑ Window Treatments	❑ ❑ Exhaust Fan(s)	❑ ❑ Fireplace Screen / Doors

Other inclusions or exclusions: _____

_____

WATER, SEWAGE, HEATING, AND CENTRAL AIR CONDITIONING: (Check all that apply)
Water Supply: ❑ Public ❑ Well ❑ Other ____ Hot Water: ❑ Oil ❑ Gas ❑ Elec.
Sewage Disposal: ❑ Public ❑ Septic # BR ____ Air Conditioning: ❑ Gas ❑ Elec. ❑ Heat Pump
Heating: ❑ Oil ❑ Gas ❑ Elec. ❑ Heat Pump ❑ Other _____

2. The Broker and the Sales Associates shall promote the interests of the Seller by: (a) performing the terms of this Agreement; (b) seeking a buyer at a price and terms agreed upon herein or otherwise acceptable to the Seller, however, the Broker and the Sales Associates shall not be obligated to seek additional offers to purchase the Property while the Property is subject to a contract of sale, unless stated below in Paragraph 19, "Other Terms" or as the contact of sale so provides; (c) presenting in a timely manner all written offers or counteroffers to and from the Seller even when the Property is already subject to a contract of sale; (d) disclosing to the Seller all material facts related to the Property or concerning the transaction of which the Broker and Sales Associate have actual knowledge; (e) accounting for in a timely manner all money and property received in which the Seller has or may have an interest. Unless otherwise provided by law or the Seller consents in writing herein or elsewhere to the release of the information, the Broker and the Sales Associate shall maintain the confidentiality of all personal and financial information and other matters identified as confidential by the Seller, if that information is received from the Seller during the brokerage relationship. In satisfying these duties, the Broker and the Sales Associate shall exercise ordinary care, comply with all applicable laws and regulations and treat all prospective buyers honestly and not knowingly give them false information; and the Broker and Sales Associate shall disclose to prospective buyers all material adverse facts pertaining to the physical condition of the Property which are actually known by them. In addition, the Broker and the Sales Associate may provide assistance to a buyer or prospective buyer by performing ministerial acts that are not inconsistent with the Broker's and the Sales Associate's duties under this Agreement. The Seller acknowledges that the Broker and Sales Associate and any cooperating brokers and sales associates may act on behalf of the Seller as the Seller's representatives.

Buyer representation occurs when buyers elect to use the services of their own broker (known as a buyer representative) to act on their behalf.

Dual representation occurs when a buyer and seller in one transaction are represented by the same Broker and the same Sales Associate. When the parties agree to dual representation, the ability of the Broker and the Sales Associate to represent either party fully and exclusively is limited. The confidentiality of all information of all clients shall be maintained as above.

Designated representation occurs when a buyer and seller in one transaction are represented by different Sales Associates affiliated with the same Broker. Each of these Sales Associates, known as a Designated Representative, represents fully the interests of a different client in the same transaction. Designated Representatives are not dual representatives if each represents only the buyer or only the seller in a specific real estate transaction. Except for disclosure of confidential information to the Broker, each Designated Representative is bound by the confidentiality requirements as above. The Broker remains a dual representative.

Dual representation: ❑ The Seller consents to dual representation OR ❑ The Seller does not consent to dual representation which means the Seller does not allow the Property to be shown to a buyer listed with the Broker through the same Sales Associate.

Designated representation: ❑ The Seller consents to designated representation OR ❑ The Seller does not consent to designated representation which means the Seller does not allow the Property to be shown to a buyer listed with the Broker through another Designated Representative associated with the firm. The Broker will notify other associates within the firm via the MLS whether the Seller consents or does not consent.

3. This Exclusive Right to Sell will expire at midnight on _____.

4. This Property shall be shown and made available without regard to race, color, religion, sex, handicap, familial status or national origin as well as all classes protected by the laws of the United States, the Commonwealth of Virginia and applicable local jurisdictions.

Rev. 2/3/99   Page 1 of 2   Please Initial: Seller ____/____ Broker ____/____

Figure 2.1   *(continued)*

5. The Broker shall make a blanket unilateral offer of cooperation and compensation to other brokers in any Multiple Listing Service that the Broker deems appropriate. The Broker shall disseminate information regarding the Property, including the entry date, listing price(s), final price and all terms, and expired or withdrawn status, by printed form and/or electronic computer service during and after the expiration of this Agreement. Further, the Broker ❑ shall, OR ❑ shall not disclose the contract price in any Multiple Listing Service prior to settlement. The Broker shall enter the listing information into the MLS data base within 48 hours (unless otherwise instructed in writing by the Seller) after all Sellers' signatures have been obtained.

6. A. The Seller shall pay the Broker compensation of _____ in cash if, during the term of this Agreement, anyone produces a buyer ready, willing and able to buy the Property. The compensation is also earned if within _____ days after the expiration or termination of this Agreement, a contract is ratified with a ready, willing and able buyer to whom the Property has been shown during the term of this Agreement; provided, however, that the compensation need not be paid if a contract is ratified on the Property while the Property is listed with another real estate company. B. The Broker acknowledges receipt of a retainer fee in the amount of _____ which ❑ shall, OR ❑ shall not be subtracted from any compensation due the Broker under this Agreement. The retainer is non-refundable and is earned when paid. C. The Broker shall offer compensation as indicated: Subagency Compensation _____ Buyer Agency Compensation

Nonagency Compensation as defined by law _____ *Note: Compensation shall be shown by a percentage of the gross selling price, a definite dollar amount or "N" for no compensation.*
The Broker has the authority to revise compensation amounts upon written notice to the Seller. ❑ Yes ❑ No

7. No Multiple Listing Service or Association of REALTORS® is a party to this Agreement and no Multiple Listing Service or Association of REALTORS® sets, controls, recommends or suggests the amount of compensation for any brokerage service rendered pursuant to this Agreement, whether by the listing broker or by any other broker acting as subagent or otherwise.

8. In consideration of the use of Broker's services and facilities and of the facilities of any REALTOR® Multiple Listing Service, the Seller and Seller's heirs and assigns hereby release the Broker, sales associates accompanying buyers or prospective buyers, any REALTORS® Multiple Listing Service and the directors, officers and employees thereof, including officials of any parent Association of REALTORS®, except for malfeasance on the part of such parties, from any liability to the Seller for vandalism, theft or damage of any nature whatsoever to the Property or its contents during the term of this Agreement, and that the Seller waives any and all rights, claims and causes of action against them and holds them harmless for any property damage or personal injury arising from the use or access to the Property by any person during the term of this Agreement.

9. Virginia licensed real estate salespersons and appraisers, inspectors or other persons may require access to the Property to facilitate and/or consummate a sale. Authorization is granted to the Broker to show the Property during reasonable hours. In the event of a sale, the Seller will sign a sales contract enforceable in the Commonwealth of Virginia.

10. The Seller retains full responsibility for the Property, including all utilities, maintenance, physical security and liability during the term of the Agreement.

11. The Seller represents that the Property ❑ is, OR ❑ is not located within a development which is a Condominium or Cooperative. Condominiums or Cooperatives being offered for sale are subject to the receipt by buyers of the required Disclosures, and the Seller is responsible for securing and furnishing these to prospective buyers as prescribed in the Condominium Act, Section 55-79.39 et seq., and the Cooperative Act, Section 55-424, et seq., of the Code of Virginia (1950).

12. The Seller represents that the Property ❑ is, OR ❑ is not located within a development which is subject to the Virginia Property Owners' Association Act, Sections 55-508 through 55-516 of the Code of Virginia (1950). If the Property is within such a development, the Act requires the development's property owner's association ("Association") to provide the Seller within 14 days of a written request and payment of the appropriate fee, with a disclosure packet which the Seller will request from the Association and provide to the buyer.

13. The Seller acknowledges that the Broker has informed the Seller of the Seller's rights and obligations under the Virginia Residential Property Disclosure Act. This Property ❑ is, OR ❑ is not exempt from the Act. If not exempt, the Seller has completed and provided to the Broker: ❑ a Residential Property Disclosure Statement where the Seller is making representations regarding the condition of the Property on which the buyer may rely, OR ❑ a Residential Property Disclaimer Statement where the Seller is making no representations regarding the condition of the Property and is selling the Property "as is", except as may be provided otherwise in the sales contract.

14. The Seller represents that the residential dwelling(s) at the Property ❑ were, OR ❑ were not constructed before 1978. If the dwelling(s) were constructed before 1978, the Seller is subject to Federal law concerning disclosure of the possible presence of lead-based paint at the Property, and the Seller acknowledges that the Broker has informed the Seller of the Seller's obligations under the law. If the dwelling(s) were constructed before 1978, unless exempt under 42 U.S.C. 4852d, the Seller has completed and provided to the Broker the form, "Sale: Disclosure And Acknowledgment Of Information On Lead-Based Paint And/Or Lead-Based Paint Hazards" or equivalent.

15. Authority is granted to the Broker to: A. Place a "For Sale" sign on the Property and to remove all other such signs and B. Place a common keysafe/lockbox on the Property containing keys necessary to obtain full access to the Property.

16. The Property may be sold subject to existing Deed(s) of Trust, having a total unpaid balance of approximately $ _____.

17. The Seller shall provide a _____ Deed of Trust Loan in the amount of $ _____ with further terms to be negotiated.

18. The Seller ❑ is, OR ❑ is not a licensed (active/inactive) real estate agent/broker.

19. Other terms: _____

The terms and conditions of this Agreement must be used as a basis for presenting the Property to prospective buyers, and, unless amended in writing, contain the final and entire Agreement between the parties hereto. The parties shall not be bound by any terms, conditions, oral statements, warranties or representations not herein contained. Seen and agreed and receipt of a signed copy of this Agreement is hereby acknowledge.

_____ Date _____ Seller   _____ Broker
                                                                                    (Firm)

_____ Date _____ Seller   _____
                                                                                    (Address)

_____   _____, VA _____
            (Seller's Mailing Address)

_____   Date _____ By: _____
            (City, State, Zip)   (Broker/Sales Manager)

                                                        Sales Associate _____
                                                                                    (Designated Representative)

BUYER REPRESENTATION

A buyer's agent establishes a brokerage relationship with a client through a *buyer representation agreement.* A typical buyer's representation agreement used in Virginia is illustrated in Figure 2.2.

STATUTE OF FRAUDS

It should be noted that while an oral listing or buyer representation agreement may be made, such an agreement would not be enforceable in Virginia.

SELLER DISCLOSURE

The Residential Property Disclosure Act [§55-517 et seq.] requires that sellers disclose all material information about the property being sold or allows the seller to file a disclaimer. The act applies to residential property consisting of one to four units, and to sales, options, installment sales or leases with option-to-buy. The law applies to the sale of most residential property, whether or not a real estate professional is involved. If a licensee is involved, the disclosure should be obtained when the listing is taken. The disclosure must be made *prior* to acceptance of an offer.

Sellers must disclose certain known information about the property (see Figure 2.3). The information includes:

- the property's age and physical condition, structural defects, termites, environmental hazards and land use issues;

- the type of water and sewage, plumbing, electrical, heating, ventilation and air conditioning (HVAC) systems; and

- type of insulation, roof condition and material.

SELLER DISCLAIMER

A seller may choose to file a *disclaimer* instead of the disclosure (see Figure 2.4). In choosing a disclaimer over the disclosure statement, the seller offers the property "as is," without any guarantees, under the doctrine of caveat emptor ("let the buyer beware"). The disclosure or disclaimer may be included in the contract itself, in an addendum to the contract or as a separate document.

Time for Disclosure

The disclosure/disclaimer is required *prior* to contract ratification by the seller and buyer. If the disclosure or disclaimer is received *after* contract ratification, the sole remedy for the purchaser is to terminate the contract by giving written notice to the seller. Once the disclosure or disclaimer is received by the buyer, notice to terminate must be given to the seller

- within three days if the notice is hand carried;

- within five days of postmark, if the notice is mailed;

- prior to settlement; or

- prior to occupancy if occupancy occurs before settlement.

The purchaser may allow the contract to remain valid if he or she

- provides a notice of waiver of rights to terminate the contract, or

- remains silent and does nothing.

If the purchaser elects to terminate the contract in accordance with the disclosure law, he or she may do so without any penalty. Any monies already paid by the purchaser (such as earnest money deposits) must be returned.

Figure 2.2   Buyer Representation Agreement

EXCLUSIVE RIGHT TO REPRESENT BUYER AGREEMENT

This Agreement is made on _____, 19 _____ between _____

_____ ("Buyer") and _____ ("Broker").
(Name of brokerage firm)

In consideration of services and facilities, the Broker is hereby granted the right to represent the Buyer in the acquisition of real property. (As used in this Agreement, "acquisition of real property" shall include any purchase, option, exchange or lease of property or an agreement to do so.)

1. BUYER'S REPRESENTATIONS. The Buyer represents that as of the commencement date of this Agreement, the Buyer is not a party to a buyer representation agreement with any other brokerage firm. The Buyer further represents that the Buyer has disclosed to the Sales Associate information about any properties that the Buyer has previously visited at any new homes communities or resale "open houses", or that the Buyer has been shown by any other real estate sales associate(s) in any area where the Buyer seeks to acquire property under this Agreement.

The Buyer ☐ does OR ☐ does not hold an active or inactive Virginia real estate license.

2. TERM. This Agreement commences when signed and, subject to Paragraph 7, terminates at _____ a.m./p.m. on _____, 19 _____.

3. RETAINER FEE. The Broker, _____, acknowledges receipt
(Name of brokerage firm)
of a retainer fee in the amount of _____, which shall be subtracted from any compensation due the Broker under this Agreement. The retainer is non-refundable and is earned when paid.

4. BROKER'S DUTIES. The Broker and the Sales Associate shall promote the interests of the Buyer by: (a) performing the terms of this Agreement; (b) seeking property at a price and terms acceptable to the Buyer; (c) presenting in a timely manner all written offers or counteroffers to and from the Buyer; (d) disclosing to the Buyer all material facts related to the property or concerning the transaction of which they have actual knowledge; (e) accounting for in an timely manner all money and property received in which the Buyer has or may have an interest. Unless otherwise provided by law or the Buyer consents in writing to the release of the information, the Broker shall maintain the confidentiality of all personal and financial information and other matters identified as confidential by the Buyer, if that information is received from the Buyer during the brokerage relationship. In satisfying these duties, the Broker shall exercise ordinary care, comply with all applicable laws and regulations, treat all prospective sellers honestly and not knowingly give them false information, and disclose whether or not the Buyer's intent is to occupy the property as a principal residence. In addition, the Broker may show the same property to other buyers, represent other buyers, represent sellers relative to other properties, or provide assistance to a seller or prospective seller by performing ministerial acts that are not inconsistent with the Broker's duties under this Agreement.

5. BUYER'S DUTIES. The Buyer shall: (a) work exclusively with the Broker during the term of this Agreement; (b) pay the Broker, directly or indirectly, the compensation set forth below; (c) comply with the reasonable requests of the Broker to supply and pertinent financial or personal data needed to fulfill the terms of this Agreement; (d) be available during the Broker's regular working hours to view properties.

6. PURPOSE. The Buyer is retaining the Broker to acquire the following type of property: _____
_____.

7. COMPENSATION. In consideration of the time and effort expended by the Broker on behalf of the Buyer, and in further consideration of the advice and counsel provided to the Buyer, the Buyer shall pay compensation ("Broker's Fee") to the Broker as described below. The Broker's Fee, less the retainer fee, if any, shall be earned, due and payable under any of these circumstances whether the transaction is consummated through the services of the Broker or otherwise:

(a) If the Buyer enters into a contract to acquire real property during the term of this Agreement and goes to settlement on that contract any time thereafter: **OR**

(b) If, within _____ days of expiration of this Agreement, the Buyer enters into a contract to acquire real property that has been described to or shown to the Buyer by the Broker during the term of this Agreement, unless the Buyer has entered into a subsequent "Exclusive Right to Represent Buyer" agreement with another real estate broker; **OR**

(c) If, having entered into a enforceable contract to acquire real property during the term of this Agreement, the Buyer defaults under the terms of that contract.

The Broker's Fee shall be _____.

If the seller or the seller's representative offers compensation to the Buyer's Broker, then the Buyer authorizes the Broker to receive such compensation and the amount of such compensation shall be credited against the Buyer's obligation to pay the Broker's Fee.

Any obligation incurred under this Agreement on the part of the Buyer to pay the Broker's Fee shall survive the term of this Agreement.

Initials: Buyer _____/ _____

Figure 2.2 *(continued)*

8. **DISCLOSED DUAL REPRESENTATION.** The Buyer acknowledges that in the normal course of business the Broker may represent seller of properties in which the Buyer is interested. If the Buyer wishes to acquire any property listed with the Broker, then the Buyer will be represented in one of the two ways that are permitted under Virginia law in this situation. The written consent required from the parties in each case will be accomplished via execution of the appropriate disclosure form at the time of the contract offer.

Dual representation occurs when a buyer and seller in one transaction are represented by the same Broker and the same Sales Associate. When the parties agree to dual representation, the ability of the Broker and the Sales Associate to represent either party fully and exclusively is limited. The confidentiality of all clients shall be maintained as in paragraph 4 above.

Designated representation occurs when a buyer and seller in one transaction are represented by different Sales Associates affiliated with the same Broker. Each of these Sales Associates, known as a Designated Representative, represents fully the interests of a different client in the same transaction. Designated Representatives are not dual representatives if each represents only the buyer or only the seller in a specific real estate transaction. Except for disclosure of confidential information to the Broker, each Designated Representative is bound by the confidentiality requirements in paragraph 4 above. The Broker remains a dual representative.

CHECK ONE CHOICE IN EACH SECTION:

> *Dual representation:* The Buyer ☐ does **OR** ☐ does not consent to be shown and to consider acquiring properties listed with the Broker through the Sales Associate.
>
> *Designated representation:* The Buyer ☐ does **OR** ☐ does not consent to be shown and to consider acquiring properties listed with the Broker through another Designated Representative associated with the firm.

9. **DISCLAIMER.** The buyer acknowledges that the Broker is being retained solely as a real estate agent and is not an attorney, tax advisor, lender, appraiser, surveyor, structural engineer, home inspector or other professional service provider. The Buyer is advised to seek professional advice concerning the condition of the property or concerning legal and tax matters.

10. **EQUAL OPPORTUNITY.** Properties shall be shown and made available to the Buyer without regard to race, color, religion, sex, handicap, familial status or national origin as well as all classes protected by the laws of the United States, the Commonwealth of Virginia and applicable local jurisdictions.

11. **OTHER PROVISIONS.** _____

_____ .

12. **MISCELLANEOUS.** This Agreement, any exhibits and any addenda signed by the parties constitute the entire agreement between the parties and supersedes any other written or oral agreements between the parties. This Agreement can only be modified in writing when signed by both parties. In any action or proceeding involving a dispute between the Buyer, the seller and/or the Broker, arising out of this Agreement, or to collect the Broker's Fee, the prevailing party shall be entitled to receive from the other party reasonable attorney's fees to be determined by the court or arbitrator(s).

(NOTE: The Buyer should consult with the Sales Associate before visiting any resale or new homes or contacting any other REALTORS® representing sellers, to avoid the possibility of confusion over the brokerage relationship and misunderstandings about liability for compensation)

_____
Brokerage Firm (Broker)

_____(SEAL)
Buyer's Signature

_____
Address

_____(SEAL)
Buyer's Signature

_____
City, State, Zip Code

_____(SEAL)
Broker/Sales Manager's Signature

_____
Address

_____
Sales Associate's/Designated Representative's Printed Name

_____
City, State, Zip Code

Telephone:_____ _____
     Work   Home

Telephone: _____ _____
     Work   Home

Figure 2.3   Residential Property Disclosure Statement

RESIDENTIAL PROPERTY DISCLOSURE STATEMENT
THIS IS NOT A WARRANTY OF THE CONDITION OF THE PROPERTY

NOTE TO OWNER(S): Complete and sign this statement only if you elect to disclose defects in the conditions of the property actually known by you; otherwise, sign the RESIDENTIAL PROPERTY DISCLAIMER STATEMENT. You may wish to obtain professional advice or inspection of the property, or obtain information from the Department of Environmental Quality which identifies confirmed releases or discharges of oil which may affect the property, but you are not required to undertake or provide any independent investigation or inspection of the property in order to make the disclosures set forth below.

NOTE TO PURCHASER(S): This statement is based upon the owner's actual knowledge of the condition of the property as of the date noted. You may wish to obtain professional advice or inspections of the property, or obtain information from the Department of Environmental Quality which identifies confirmed releases or discharges of oil which may affect the property. The information contained in this statement is the representation of the owner and not the representation of the broker or salesperson, if any.

Property Address/Legal Description: _____

How long have you owned the property? _____   Dates lived in property? _____

Property Systems: Water, Sewage, Heating & Air Conditioning (Answer all that apply)

Water Supply	☐ Public ☐ Well ☐ Other _____			
Sewage Disposal	☐ Public ☐ Septic System approved for ____ (#) BR	Garbage Disposal ☐ Yes ☐ No	Dishwasher ☐ Yes ☐ No	
Heating	☐ Oil ☐ Natural Gas ☐ Electric	☐ Heat Pump	Age _____	Other _____
Air Conditioning	☐ Oil ☐ Natural Gas ☐ Electric	☐ Heat Pump	Age _____	Other _____
Hot Water	☐ Oil ☐ Natural Gas ☐ Electric	Capacity _____	Age _____	Other _____

Please indicate your actual knowledge with respect to the following:

1. **Structural Systems, including Roof, Walls, Floors, Foundation and any Basement: Any known defects (structural or otherwise)?**
   ☐ Yes ☐ No ☐ Unknown
   Comments: _____

2. **Basement: Any leaks or evidence of moisture?**
   ☐ Yes ☐ No ☐ Unknown ☐ Does Not Apply
   Comments: _____

3. **Roof: Any leaks or evidence of moisture?**
   ☐ Yes ☐ No ☐ Unknown
   Type of roof: _____ Age _____
   Is there any existing fire retardant treated (FRT) plywood?
   ☐ Yes ☐ No ☐ Unknown ☐ Does Not Apply
   Comments: _____

4. **Fireplace/Chimney(s): In working condition?**
   ☐ Yes ☐ No ☐ Unknown ☐ Does Not Apply
   Comments: _____

5. **Plumbing System: Is the system in working condition?**
   ☐ Yes ☐ No ☐ Unknown
   Comments: _____

6. **Septic/Sewer Systems: Is the System functioning properly?**
   ☐ Yes ☐ No ☐ Unknown ☐ Does Not Apply
   If septic, when was the system last pumped? _____

7. **Water Supply: Any problems with water quality or supply?**
   ☐ Yes ☐ No ☐ Unknown
   Is the system in working condition?
   ☐ Yes ☐ No ☐ Unknown
   Comments: _____

8. **Heating System: Is heat supplied to all finished rooms?**
   ☐ Yes ☐ No ☐ Unknown
   Is the system in working condition?
   ☐ Yes ☐ No ☐ Unknown
   Comments: _____

9. **Air Conditioning system: Is cooling supplied to all finished rooms?**
   ☐ Yes ☐ No ☐ Unknown ☐ Does Not Apply
   Is the system in working condition?
   ☐ Yes ☐ No ☐ Unknown ☐ Does Not Apply
   Comments: _____

10. **Electric System: Are there any problems with electrical fuses/circuit breakers, outlets or wiring?**
    ☐ Yes ☐ No ☐ Unknown
    Comments: _____
    Does the electrical system meet existing code requirements?
    ☐ Yes ☐ No ☐ Unknown
    Comments: _____

11. **Insulation:**
    In exterior walls?   ☐ Yes ☐ No ☐ Unknown
    In ceiling/attic?   ☐ Yes ☐ No ☐ Unknown
    In other areas?   ☐ Yes ☐ No ☐ Unknown
    Comments: _____

12. **Exterior Drainage: Does water stand on the property for more than 24 hours after a heavy rain?**
    ☐ Yes ☐ No ☐ Unknown
    Are gutters and downspouts in working condition?
    ☐ Yes ☐ No ☐ Unknown ☐ Does Not Apply
    Comments: _____

13. **Wood-destroying organisms: Any infestation and/or prior damage?**
    ☐ Yes ☐ No ☐ Unknown
    Any treatments or repairs?
    ☐ Yes ☐ No ☐ Unknown
    Comments: _____

14. **Are there any substances, materials or environmental hazards (including, but not limited to asbestos, radon gas, lead-based paint, underground storage tanks, or other contamination) on or affecting the property?**
    ☐ Yes ☐ No ☐ Unknown
    Comments: _____

15. **Are there any additions, structural modifications or other alterations or repairs made without required permits or not in compliance with building codes?**
    ☐ Yes ☐ No ☐ Unknown
    Comments: _____

16. **Are there any zoning violations, nonconforming uses, violations of building restrictions or setback requirements, or any recorded or unrecorded easements, except for utilities, on or affecting the property?**
    ☐ Yes ☐ No ☐ Unknown
    Comments: _____

17. **Are there any defects in the following, if installed in the property?**
    Water treatment system
    ☐ Yes ☐ No ☐ Unknown ☐ Does Not Apply
    Comments: _____
    Lawn sprinkler system
    ☐ Yes ☐ No ☐ Unknown ☐ Does Not Apply
    Comments: _____
    Security system
    ☐ Yes ☐ No ☐ Unknown ☐ Does Not Apply
    Comments: _____

18. **Are there any other material defects affecting the physical condition of the property?**
    ☐ Yes ☐ No ☐ Unknown
    Comments: _____

19. **Is the property subject to covenants and restrictions, the VA Condominium Act, VA Property Owners Association Act or Real Estate Cooperative Act?**
    ☐ Yes ☐ No ☐ Unknown
    Comments: _____

Note: Owner(s) may wish to disclose the condition of other buildings on the property on a separate RESIDENTIAL PROPERTY DISCLOSURE STATEMENT.

Note: Purchaser(s) should exercise whatever due diligence they deem necessary with respect to information on any sexual offenders registered under Chapter 23 (

◆◆

The owner(s) acknowledge having carefully examined this statement, including any comments continued on the reverse side, and state that this statement is complete and accurate as of the date signed. At or before settlement, the owner(s) will be required to disclose any material change in the physical condition of the property. The owner(s) further acknowledge that they have been informed of their rights and obligations under the Virginia Residential Property Disclosure Act.

_____   _____   _____   _____
Owner   Date   Owner   Date

The purchaser(s) acknowledge receipt of a copy of this disclosure statement and further acknowledge that they have been informed of their rights and obligations under the Virginia Residential Property Disclosure Act. The purchaser(s) acknowledge that the owner(s) make no representation with respect to any matters which may pertain to parcels adjacent to the subject property and should exercise whatever due diligence deemed necessary with respect to adjacent parcels in accordance with terms and conditions as may be contained in the real estate purchase contract, but in any event, prior to settlement.

_____   _____   _____   _____
Purchaser   Date   Purchaser   Date

Figure 2.4   Residential Property Disclaimer Statement

RESIDENTIAL PROPERTY DISCLAIMER STATEMENT

NOTICE TO SELLER AND PURCHASER

The Virginia Residential Property Disclosure Act requires the owner of certain residential real property, whenever the property is to be sold or leased with an option to buy, to furnish to the purchaser either (a) a RESIDENTIAL PROPERTY DISCLAIMER STATEMENT stating that the owner makes no representations or warranties as to the condition of the property, except as otherwise provided in the purchase contract, or (b) a RESIDENTIAL PROPERTY DISCLOSURE STATEMENT disclosing defects in the condition of the property actually known by the owner. Certain transfers of residential property are excluded from this requirement (see the exemptions listed on the reverse side).

◆◆◆◆◆◆◆◆◆◆◆◆◆◆◆◆◆◆◆◆◆◆◆◆◆◆◆◆◆◆◆◆◆◆◆◆◆◆◆

RESIDENTIAL PROPERTY DISCLAIMER STATEMENT

NOTE TO OWNER(S): Sign this statement only if you elect to sell the property without representations and warranties as to its conditions, except as otherwise provided in the purchase contract; otherwise, complete and sign the RESIDENTIAL PROPERTY DISCLOSURE STATEMENT.

Property Address/
Legal Description: _____

The undersigned owner(s) of the real property described above make no representations or warranties as to the condition of the real property or any improvements thereon, and the purchaser will be receiving the property "as is", that is, with all defects which may exist, if any, except as otherwise provided in the real estate purchase contract.

The owner(s) acknowledge having carefully examined this statement and further acknowledge that they have been informed of their rights and obligations under the Virginia Residential Property Disclosure Act.

_____ _____   _____ _____
    Owner   Date   Owner   Date

NOTE TO PURCHASER(S): The owner(s) make no representations with respect to any matters which may pertain to parcels adjacent to the subject parcel. You should exercise whatever due diligence you deem necessary with respect to adjacent parcels in accordance with the terms and conditions as may be contained in the real estate purchase contract, but in any event, prior to settlement. You should exercise whatever due diligence you deem necessary with respect to information on any sexual offenders registered under Chapter 23 (§19.2-387 et seq.) of Title 19.2, whether the owner proceeds under subdivision 1 or 2 of subsection A of §55-519. Such information may be obtained by contacting your local police department or the Department of State Police, Central Criminal Records Exchange, at 804-674-2000 or www.state.va.us/vsp/vsp.html.

The purchaser(s) acknowledge receipt of a copy of this disclaimer statement and further acknowledge that they have been informed of their rights and obligations under the Virginia Residential Property Disclosure Act.

_____ _____   _____ _____
    Purchaser   Date   Purchaser   Date

DPOR 1/1/99

The purchaser will lose the right to terminate the contract if the termination right is not exercised

- at the time the purchaser makes a written application to obtain a mortgage loan, and the loan application contains a disclosure that the right to terminate shall end; *or*

- at settlement or occupancy, in the event of a sale; *or*

- at the time of occupancy in the event of lease with option to buy.

Builders of new homes must only disclose known material defects that would constitute a violation of local building codes. Builders are required to disclose defects before acceptance of an offer for purchase of an already completed house or after issuance of an occupancy permit if the offer is accepted before or during construction.

The issuance of the disclosure does not relieve the builder of any other new home warranties or contractual obligations. While the disclosure may be in any form, the builder may *not* satisfy the disclosure requirement by the use of the disclaimer statement.

Megan's Law

Disclosure and disclaimer forms must contain a notice advising purchasers that they should exercise whatever due diligence they deem necessary with respect to information on violent sexual offenders registered with the Commonwealth. The form is not required for new home sales, transfers involving trusts, foreclosures or residential leases. However, it is advocated that new disclosure language be added to all contracts and agency agreements.

Exemptions

Certain transactions are exempt from the disclosure requirements. These include

- court-ordered transfers
  - to settle an estate;
  - pursuant to a writ of execution;
  - foreclosures;
  - by a trustee in bankruptcy;
  - by condemnation through the right of eminent domain; and
  - by suit for specific performance.

- voluntary transfers of property
  - between co-owners;
  - between relatives;
  - under a divorce settlement;
  - to or from any governmental entity or public or quasi-public housing authority or agency;
  - as the result of an owner's failure to pay federal, state or local taxes; and
  - involving the first sale of a new home, except as exempted.

Buyer's Recourse

If the buyer learns of defects that either were not disclosed or were misrepresented in the disclosure statement, the buyer is entitled to seek recourse. Any action brought under this act must be commenced within one year from the date the disclosure was delivered. If no disclosure was delivered, action must be commenced within one year of settlement (or within one year of occupancy in the event of a lease with option to buy).

The owner is not liable for any error, inaccuracy or omission of information in the disclosure form if the information was provided to the owner by a *reliable third party* such as a surveyor, engineer, appraiser, home inspector or public authority. The owner is also not liable if he or she *reasonably believed the information to be correct* and there was no gross negligence involved.

Licensee Liability

Like the owner, a real estate licensee cannot be liable for misrepresentation if he or she relied on information provided by others. However, a licensee must disclose material adverse facts pertaining to the physical condition of the property that are actually known by the licensee. [§54.1-2131B; Regs. 135-20-300(4)]

FOR EXAMPLE...

T, a real estate salesperson, is hosting an open house during a rainstorm. While no one is being shown the property, *T* notices that there is a leak in the attic and water seepage in the basement. *T* must disclose that information to any prospective buyers, even if the owner knowingly falsified the disclosure statement or filed a disclaimer because he or she did not want to admit that anything was wrong. If *T* fails to inform a prospective buyer about the leaking and seepage, *T* may be found guilty of misrepresentation.

STIGMATIZED PROPERTY

Stigmatized property refers to any property that is made undesirable by some event or circumstance that had no actual effect on its physical structure, environment or improvements. For instance, a house in which a homicide, felony or suicide occurred may be "tainted" by that event, and be difficult to sell. Buyers may hesitate to make an offer on a property that is reputed to be haunted, or in which the current or former occupant suffered from a communicable disease.

Virginia has specifically addressed the matter of stigmatized properties in the Residential Property Disclosure Act. Disclosure of this type of information, which in Virginia has been determined to be immaterial, is *not* required. In fact, a licensee who represents a seller and discloses stigmatizing information to a buyer could be construed as having breached his or her responsibilities to the client if the buyer cancels the contract due to the disclosure. The failure to disclose this information does not subject either the owner or a licensee to disciplinary action by the courts or the REB.

IN PRACTICE...
If information is disclosed regarding persons infected with HIV, a licensee could be in violation of fair housing laws and the federal Privacy Act.

LIABILITY AND IMPUTED KNOWLEDGE

Under Virginia's agency statute, a client, (whether a buyer or seller) is not liable for any misrepresentations made by a broker. [54.1-2142] The statute expressly abolishes common law concepts of vicarious liability and imputed knowledge. That is, clients and licensees are presumed to possess actual knowledge of information only. The fact that a licensee is aware of a fact does not lead to the presumption that the client is also aware of it. However, if the client knows (or should have known) that a licensee is spreading false or misleading information, he or she is obliged to take "reasonable steps" to correct the misrepresentation in a timely manner. A client is also not liable for the negligence, gross negligence or intentional acts of any broker or broker's licensee.

Similarly, a broker who enlists another broker to assist in providing brokerage services to a client is not liable for that broker's misrepresentations unless he or she knew or should have known about them and failed to take reasonable corrective steps. A broker is not liable for the negligence, gross negligence or intentional acts of an assisting broker or the assisting broker's licensee.

Both clients and licensees are fully liable for their own misrepresentations, negligence, gross negligence or intentional acts in connection with a real estate transaction.

Questions

1. When a broker and seller enter into an exclusive-right-to-sell listing, which of the following is required?

   a. Net amount seller receives at closing
   b. Definite termination date
   c. Extension or protective clause
   d. Statement of the exact acreage or square footage of the parcel or lot

2. A seller offers you a listing agreement that contains the following clause:

   Seller must receive the amount of $60,000 from the sale of this property. Seller agrees that the selling agent will receive, as his or her total compensation, any proceeds that remain beyond that amount after satisfaction of seller's mortgage loan and any closing costs incurred by seller.

   Under these facts, you

   a. must decline this listing agreement because the clause violates REB regulations.
   b. must decline this listing agreement because it is not the standard form used in Virginia.
   c. may accept this listing agreement because the clause is standard in an open listing.
   d. may accept this listing agreement, because it specifically limits the amount of your compensation.

3. A seller's home is over 80 years old, and its plumbing and wiring systems have never been replaced, repaired or upgraded. Which of the following statements is true?

   a. The seller is required by Virginia law to disclose the property's age and the condition of its plumbing and wiring.
   b. Under the doctrine of caveat emptor, the seller is required to disclose the information to a prospective buyer at the time an offer is made.
   c. The seller may file a disclaimer instead of a disclosure, offering the property "as is."
   d. The disclosures may be made at any time prior to closing.

4. A real estate broker representing the seller knows that the property has a cracked foundation and that its former owner committed suicide in the kitchen. The broker must disclose

   a. both facts.
   b. the suicide, but not the foundation.
   c. the cracked foundation, but disclosing the suicide could constitute a breach of duty to the client.
   d. neither fact.

5. All of the following are exempt from the Residential Property Disclosure Act EXCEPT

   a. a foreclosure sale.
   b. a sale by an uncle to his niece.
   c. conveyance of a primary residence from one former spouse to another under a divorce settlement agreement.
   d. a sale by a real estate licensee of a two-unit residential property.

3 Intersts in Real Estate

EMINENT DOMAIN

In Virginia, the power of eminent domain is provided by the state constitution and statutes. Virginia law provides that easements, ingress and egress rights, flowage rights and all similar rights and uses constitute "property." As a result, *just compensation* must be paid if they are taken or damaged by the Commonwealth through the power of eminent domain (sometimes referred to as a *taking*). This process is called *condemnation*.

Just compensation means the fair market value of the property at the time of the taking. Payment of just compensation is a prerequisite to passing of title to the property. In addition, the Commonwealth must have made a genuine but ineffectual effort to purchase the property directly before beginning condemnation proceedings.

If the parties do not agree on what constitutes just compensation for the land, commissioners are appointed to hold a hearing and determine the amount. Virginia's Condemnation Act provides for a two-stage proceeding. First, the court determines the fair market value of the land taken and the damage (if any) to the remaining land. Second, if payment occurs, the court determines the rights and claims of all persons entitled to compensation.

Disclosure

Real estate licensees are required to disclose to all interested parties that a parcel or an entire area is planned for condemnation. If a seller is aware that a governmental authority has made an offer to acquire the property, and that condemnation proceedings are contemplated, prospective buyers should be made aware of this information. Because condemnation can affect the value of both the condemned property as well as neighboring properties, it is an important consideration for buyers and sellers alike.

FOR EXAMPLE . . .

O's property was condemned for street construction. This had an adverse impact on the value of *O*'s remaining property. However, the value of adjacent parcels increased as a result of the improved access provided by the street.

ESTATES IN LAND

Virginia recognizes all the major estates in land, such as fee simple and life estates; defeasible and determinable estates; and remainders, reversions and the possibility of reverter.

DESCENT AND DISTRIBUTION AND MARITAL ESTATES

In 1991, the Virginia legislature abolished the concepts of dower and curtesy.

The Augmented Estate and Elective Share Act [§64.1] defines to whom a deceased person's property is distributed if he or she dies *intestate* (without having executed a valid will). Commonly referred to as the *law of descent and distribution*, this statute is similar to the old dower and curtesy statutes because it establishes the rights of ownership to property by a surviving spouse and others.

NOTE: *The following discussion is only an overview of this complex law.*

Intestate Distributions

The Act defines the rights of natural children, adopted children, children by previous marriages, illegitimate children, children of surrogates and children born by in vitro fertilization. Real estate licensees are cautioned that their involvement in real estate transactions involving part of an estate can open the door to complications that may arise from claims by the heirs.

If a person dies testate (that is, having executed a valid will), but fails to specifically devise or bequeath all of his or her property, the undistributed property is treated as if the person died intestate. It is distributed to heirs in accordance with the rules of descent and distribution.

The statute defines *property* or *estate* as including

- insurance policies,

- retirement benefits (exclusive of Social Security),

- annuities,

- pension plans and deferred compensation arrangements and

- employee benefit plans.

The surviving spouse receives one-third of this surplus. The remaining two-thirds is then distributed among the decedent's children or their descendants. If there are no children, the surviving spouse is entitled to receive the entire surplus.

FOR EXAMPLE . . .

D died without having made a valid will. *D*'s estate, valued at $785,950, was distributed among *D*'s surviving spouse and *D*'s three children (*X*, *Y* and *Z*) as follows:

> *D's surviving spouse:* $261,983.33
> *X, Y and Z:* $174,655.55 to each

If *D* had left a valid will disposing of $500,000 of the estate, the remaining $285,950 would be distributed to *D*'s spouse and children as follows:

> *D's surviving spouse:* $95,316.67
> *X, Y and Z:* $63,544.44 to each

Augmented Estate

Although a surviving spouse could be named in a will to receive certain property and to be further entitled to receive a share of the surplus, it is possible for the spouse to renounce the will and claim an *elective share* of the augmented estate.

An augmented estate consists of the property (both real and personal) owned by the deceased at the time of death. To this is added the value of property transferred during the marriage to third parties without the consent of the surviving spouse, if it can be established that the decedent did not receive adequate and full consideration for the property transferred. The value of the augmented estate is the value that remains after the payment of funeral expenses, the cost of the estate administrator and personal debts of the decedent.

Other items that could be excluded from the augmented estate include

- property owned by the surviving spouse;

- property owned by the decedent and another, with right of survivorship;

- property conveyed during the marriage with the consent of the surviving spouse;

- property acquired, by the decedent, in severalty, as a gift, by will or intestate succession from someone other than the surviving spouse; and

- property transferred prior to January 1, 1991, if such transfer was irrevocable as of that date.

If a claim for an elective share is made, the surviving spouse receives one-third of the estate if there are children. If there are no children, or descendants of children, the surviving spouse is entitled to one-half of the estate. [§64.1-16]

A surviving spouse has the right to possess and occupy the principal family residence during the period of time that the estate matters are being settled, although the residence may be a part of the augmented estate of the deceased.

Abandonment

If a husband or wife willfully deserts or abandons his or her spouse until the death of the deserted spouse, the deserting spouse is barred from all interest of the other by intestate succession, elective share, exempt property, family allowance and homestead allowance.

HOMESTEAD EXEMPTION

Under Virginia's homestead exemption, a householder is entitled to hold a certain amount of real or personal property exempt from unsecured debts. The total value of the property may not exceed $5,000, plus $500 for each dependent.

Only a householder or head of a family may have the benefit of the homestead exemption. A husband and wife living together may both be deemed householders if each contributes to maintaining the household.

The exemption does not apply against

- claims for the purchase price of the homestead property;

- mechanics' liens; and

- claims for taxes.

The claim to homestead must be made by deed (in the case of real property) or by an inventory under oath (for personal property). The owner of the homestead may sell or encumber the homestead property.

The key words in the homestead exemption are *unsecured debts*. For instance, a credit card balance is an unsecured debt. On the other hand, a mortgage or a deed of trust is secured by real property, and so has priority over the homestead exemption. The property may be sold at foreclosure to satisfy a secured debt.

In addition to the homestead estate, the householder is entitled to hold certain other items of real and personal property exempt from sale for the satisfaction of a debt, such as a family Bible; wedding and engagement rings; and a burial plot.

In certain circumstances, other items such as personal clothing, household furnishings, photographs, health aids and occupational tools also may be declared exempt.

IN PRACTICE...
A real estate agent may be unaware that a homestead deed has been filed. The exemption is usually revealed in a title search conducted by an attorney or title examiner. The agent should be aware that the filing could indicate financial difficulties or even pending bankruptcy, or that judgments may be recorded.

EASEMENTS

Creating an Easement

An easement may be acquired by express grant or may be created by covenant or agreement. In Virginia, the owner of a dominant tenement may convey the land without the easement. Where the easement is not an easement by necessity (that is, not necessary for access to the property), and the appurtenance is expressly excluded by the grant, it will not convey. When a grantor conveys land by a deed that describes the property as bounded by a road or street that the grantor owns, the grantor is implying that a right-of-way exists. The grantee acquires the benefit of the easement automatically.

If the width of a right-of-way is not specified in the grant, it is limited to the width as it existed at the time of the grant. If an easement has a definite location, it may be changed with the express or implied consent of the interested parties. The change may also be implied by the parties' actions.

If the grantor reserves an easement in the property conveyed, the reservation must be expressly stated.

Easement by Prescription

An *easement by prescription* is similar to the acquisition of property by adverse possession. In an action to establish an easement by prescription in Virginia, the court must find that the use of the property was

- adverse;

- under a claim of right;

- exclusive;

- continuous;

- uninterrupted; and

- with the knowledge and acquiescence of the landowner.

In Virginia, the prescriptive period is 20 years. *Tacking* — combining successive periods of continuous uninterrupted use by different parties — is permitted in Virginia.

When an easement is terminated, no document needs to be recorded in the clerk's office of the county where the land is located.

Questions

1. Which of the following does *not* constitute the exercise of eminent domain?

   a. A county taking a farmer's cropland for a highway
   b. The state taking from a private woodland for the construction of a roadside visitor center
   c. A county zoning ordinance change
   d. Port Authority of Hampton Roads taking riparian rights for a pier

2. For condemnation purposes, *just compensation* means

   a. fair market value at the time of the taking.
   b. fair market value at the time of purchase by the current owner.
   c. fair market value less court costs and attorneys' fees.
   d. a statutory percentage of fair market value.

3. What must happen before a condemnation suit is initiated?

   a. The owner and the government must agree.
   b. A genuine but ineffective effort to purchase must be made.
   c. The owner must have the property appraised.
   d. A statement of alternative solutions to the taking must be supplied to the owner by the condemning authority.

4. *P* is a single parent of three young children. *P*'s house is worth $75,000. What is the total maximum value of *P*'s homestead exemption?

   a. $5,000
   b. $6,500
   c. $70,000
   d. $75,000

5. What is the status of dower and curtesy rights in Virginia?

   a. Dower and curtesy have been abolished.
   b. Dower is a fee simple estate; curtesy is a life estate.
   c. Dower and curtesy are identical rights in fee simple.
   d. Dower and curtesy have been combined by statute into one right.

6. Which of the following statements concerning the homestead exemption is correct?

   a. Exemption is automatic, every homeowner has one.
   b. The homeowner's filing for homestead exemption may indicate financial difficulties.
   c. The exemption is protection against claims for taxes, mechanics' liens and deeds of trust against the property.
   d. The $5,000 exemption includes the family Bible, a wedding ring and a burial plot.

7.   All of the following are true of an easement by necessity *EXCEPT*:

a.   it must be an appurtenant easement.
b.   both the dominant and the servient
estates must have at some time in
the past been owned by the same
person.
c.   the only reasonable means of access
is over the servient estate.
d.   inconvenience is a basis for the
easement.

8.   *G* has a ten-foot easement through *H*'s for-
ested lot for the purpose of walking to the
bank of the Otter River. *G* widens the path
to 14 feet to accommodate his truck so he
can launch his boat. *H* is furious. Which of
the following is true in this situation?

a.   *G*'s original use was a right; *H* can
do nothing.
b.   The new use is hostile, and if not
stopped within 20 years, it could
become an easement by prescription.
c.   The additional four feet is a reasonable extension of the original easement and must be granted.
d.   If *G* uses the extension for 15 years,
the original easement is his by adverse possession.

4 Forms of Real Estate Ownership

CO-OWNERSHIP

Tenancy in Common

In Virginia, *tenancy in common* may be created by

- an *express limitation* to two or more persons to hold land as tenants in common;

- a *grant* of part interest in one's land to another;

- a *devise or grant* of land to two or more persons to be divided between them;

- a *breakup* of estates in joint tenancy; and

- the *dissolving* of a tenancy by the entirety as a result of the divorce or mutual agreement of the parties.

A tenant in common may convey his or her undivided interest; however, a contract by one tenant in common relating to the whole estate is voidable by any co-tenant who did not join in the contract.

A deceased co-tenant's interest, in passing through his or her will or to his or her heirs, is subject to the statute of Wills and Decedents Estates, which protects the rights of the surviving spouse (see "Augmented Estates" in Chapter 3). Tenancy in common carries no right of sur-

vivorship, and the interest of the deceased does not automatically pass to a surviving co-tenant.

Joint Tenancy

Virginia's joint tenancy is similar to that of most other states, insofar as the four unities of time, title, interest and possession must be present. However, Virginia's interpretation of *unity of interest* is that one joint tenant cannot be a tenant for life and another for years. Similarly, one tenant cannot be a tenant in fee and another a tenant for life. Joint tenancy is always created by an act of the parties, never by descent or operation of law.

The doctrine of *automatic survivorship* has been abolished in Virginia. The legislature intended to place joint tenants in the same situation as tenants in common as far as augmented estates were concerned. If the deed *expressly* creates a joint tenancy with right of survivorship, as at common law, then on the death of a joint tenant the entire estate continues in the surviving tenant or tenants. The surviving spouse of the deceased joint tenant has no liability, and the deceased's creditors have no claim against the enlarged interests of the surviving tenants. Property owners who wish to have a property pass at their death to particular persons, frequently create a joint tenancy as a substitute for a will.

A tenant in common or a joint tenant who commits waste may be liable to the other co-tenant(s) for damages. By statute, a joint tenant or a tenant in common may demand an accounting from a co-tenant who receives more than his or her fair share of rents and profits from the property. Similarly, joint tenants or tenants in common who improve a common property at their own expense are entitled to file a partition suit to divide and sell the property in order to obtain compensation for the improvements. However, if one tenant makes improvements without the consent of the other, the amount of compensation is limited to the amount by which the value of the common property has been enhanced.

Tenancy by the Entirety

Tenancy by the entirety is a special type of joint tenancy created between husband and wife. There is no right to partition or to convey a half interest. The tenancy is indestructible except by mutual agreement or divorce, in which case the tenancy by the entirety is converted into a tenancy in common.

Property held by husband and wife as tenants by the entirety is legally an asset of both parties. If one spouse contracts to convey the property, he or she cannot do so alone. The conveying spouse would be answerable to the would-be purchaser for the inability to perform.

> ### IN PRACTICE . . .
> If a married woman has retained her maiden name, the deed should grant to, for example, "John Doe and Mary Jones, husband and wife, as tenants by the entirety," *not* to "Mary Doe, also known as Mary Jones."

Neither spouse alone may encumber the property. Any debts that could become liens on the property must be entered into jointly by both parties.

Community Property

There are no community property laws in Virginia.

LAND TRUST

Land trusts are permitted in Virginia. A *land trust* is a trust in which the assets consist of real estate. While the deed to a trustee may appear to confer full powers to deal with the real property and complete legal and equitable title to the trust property, the trustee's powers are in fact restricted by a trust agreement mentioned in the deed. The agreement typically gives the beneficiary full powers of management and control. However, even the beneficiary cannot deal with the property as if no trust existed. Land trusts generally continue for a definite term.

TENANCY IN PARTNERSHIP

A partnership may own real property, but each individual partner's interest is considered personal property. A partner is co-owner with the other partners of real property as a *tenant in partnership*.

Tenancy in partnership has the following features:

- A partner (subject to the partnership agreement) has an equal right with the other partners to possess the property for partnership purposes, but may not possess it for any other purpose without the other partners' consent.

- A partner's right in a property is not assignable unless all the partners assign their rights in the same property.

- A partner's right in the property is not subject to creditors, except for a claim against the partnership itself. When partnership property is attached for a partnership debt, no rights can be claimed under homestead exemption laws by any partner or by the representative of a deceased partner.

- On the death of a partner, his or her interest in partnership property passes to the surviving partners. If the decedent was the last surviving partner, his or her right in the property vests in his or her legal representative. The surviving partners, or legal representative, have no right to possess the property for anything other than a partnership purpose.

- A partner can transfer property on behalf of all the partners if acting within the scope of the firm's business and purposes. Partners may transfer partnership property among themselves, provided all partners consent.

IN PRACTICE . . .

Whenever a real estate licensee represents a buyer who is purchasing partnership-owned property, the licensee should have an attorney review the partnership agreement to ensure that a general partner with power to bind all other general partners executes conveyance. It is desirable to have a written resolution of the partnership authorizing the sale.

CORPORATIONS

A corporation may acquire and convey real property in its corporate name. A contract entered into by a corporation under an assumed name may be enforced by either party. If an instrument bears both a corporate seal and the signatures of the responsible corporate officers, it is presumed to be a corporate instrument, even if it lacks the required number of signatures or the corporate name.

IN PRACTICE . . .

Anyone who purchases real estate from a corporation should require a written corporate resolution that duly authorizes the sale of property by the corporation.

COOPERATIVE OWNERSHIP

Cooperative ownership is governed by the Real Estate Cooperative Act. [§55-424] A *cooperative* is "real estate owned by an association, each of the members of which is entitled, by virtue of his [or her] ownership interest in the association, to exclusive possession of a unit."

Cooperative possession is evidenced by a proprietary lease. A cooperative has common elements and *limited* common elements; it is created by a *declaration of cooperative*, filed in the clerk's office of the circuit court in the district in which the real estate is located.

The cooperative association may adopt and amend bylaws, rules and regulations; adopt and amend budgets; hire and discharge management agents; regulate the use, maintenance and repair of common elements; impose charges; and exercise other powers conferred by the declaration and bylaws.

Sale of a Cooperative Interest

Before the contract for the sale of a cooperative interest is executed, the purchaser must be given (among other things) a proprietary lease, a copy of the declaration and bylaws, a copy of the rules and regulations of the association and a certificate that shows the following:

- A statement disclosing the effect of any right of first refusal or other restraint on transferability

- A statement of the amount of the monthly common expense assessment, as well as any unpaid expense currently due or payable from the sale and from the lessee

- A statement of any other fees payable by proprietary lessees

- A statement of any capital expenditures anticipated by the association for the current and next two succeeding fiscal years

- A statement of the amount of reserves for capital expenditures designated for specific projects

- The most recent regularly prepared balance sheet and income/expense statement, if any, of the association

- The current operating budget of the association and other pertinent information

IN PRACTICE . . .
In the sale of a cooperative interest, it is the seller's obligation to provide a buyer with the required information. The real estate licensee, however, is often asked to obtain the information as a service to the client.

Buyer's Right to Rescind

In Virginia, purchasers of a cooperative interest have certain rights to rescind the contract. There are two types of rescission rights: initial sale rescission and resale rescission. In an *initial sale* (the first time the cooperative interest is sold after the cooperative is established), the buyer has the right to rescind within ten days following ratification of the contract or after receiving the public offering statement, whichever is later. When a cooperative unit is *resold* (that is, from an owner to a buyer), the purchaser has the right to rescind within five days of contract ratification or receipt of the resale certificate, whichever is later.

CONDOMINIUM OWNERSHIP

The Real Estate Board is charged with the administrative responsibility for the Virginia Condominium Act. [§55-79.39]

A condominium can be a multiunit structure, town home or single-family dwelling. Even commercial properties may be condominiums. The owner of property may convert his or her property to condominium status. The owner is referred to as the *declarant* because he or she must *declare* his or her intent to have the property considered a condominium.

The declarant must provide declaration instruments to the REB that include the following:

- The name of the condominium (the name must include the word *condominium*)

- The legal description of the property

- Plats and/or plans that identify each unit

- An exact description of the horizontal and vertical boundaries of each unit

- The designation and description of common elements and limited common elements

- The exact allocation of the undivided ownership interest in the common elements

- If the property is being converted from rental property, the name of each current lessee and the date their leases expire

- Any easements that exist or that will be created

- An exact description of any proposed alterations to any existing units or common elements

In addition, the declarant must submit a copy of the *bylaws* under which the condominium will operate. The bylaws shall be specific regarding such issues as

- the form of self-governance for the unit owners;

- whether there are to be trustees, a board of directors or other officers; their exact duties and the means by which they are to be appointed or elected;

- the extent to which the governing or executive body may delegate responsibilities to a management agent;

- the accounting and management records that will be maintained;

- a schedule of meetings of all owners and of the executive body;

- statutory requirements for meeting notices (21 days); and

- the rules and regulations that will apply to all owners.

Public Offering Statement

The declarant must also provide a public offering statement (POS). The POS includes all declaration documentation and bylaws, as well as

- the name of the declarant;

- a narrative description of the condominium, including the number of units and future plans for the addition of more units;

- copies of the bylaws and any current management contracts, including a statement of the relationship between the declarant and the contractor(s);

- a statement of the overall status of any construction or improvements;

- any encumbrances, liens or easements that affect the title;

- the terms and conditions of any financing offered to purchasers;

- a statement of warranties, of the declarant's obligation to complete planned improvements, and a statement identifying the common elements and any user fees.

Sale of a Condominium Unit

At the *initial sale* of a condominium unit, the purchaser receives a copy of the POS along with the sales contract. The first purchaser of a condominium unit has the right to rescind a ratified contract, without penalty, within ten days, for any reason. The ten-day period begins with the date of contract ratification or on receipt of the POS, whichever is later.

At closing, the purchaser acquires a fee simple interest in the individual unit and an *undivided percentage interest* in the common elements as a tenant in common with the other unit owners. At this time the purchaser assumes responsibility for the individual unit purchased.

The declarant remains responsible for all unsold units, and for the overall management and maintenance of the condominium development until 75 percent of the units are sold. At that point, responsibility for maintenance and management of the property shifts to the owners' association. The declarant becomes a member of the association as owner of the remaining units.

Voting Rights

Each unit owner has an assigned ownership interest and voting rights in the governance of the condominium. This interest is usually in proportion to the size of each individual unit and the amenities of the unit. The exact percentage of ownership interest is established in the declaration.

Bylaw Changes

The Condominium Act states that 66⅔ percent of the total voting interest is required to change the bylaws.

Termination

Once a property has been declared a condominium, its status can be changed by abandoning or dissolving it. Eighty percent of the voting interest must approve the termination of a condominium's status.

Statutory Lien Rights

The unit owners' association has a statutory lien on every unit for unpaid assessments levied against the unit. This lien is secondary to real estate tax liens and other liens recorded prior to the filing of the original condominium declaration.

Resale of a Condominium Unit

All unit owners have the right to resell their individual units. In the event of an intended resale, the seller must obtain certain documents from the unit owners' association. The documents must be provided to the prospective buyer prior to contract date. The documents include:

- a copy of the most recent budget and financial reports of the association;

- a listing of anticipated capital expenditures for the current or two succeeding fiscal years;

- current assessments and any other fees levied on the unit owners;

- the amount set aside for specific projects, replacement or repairs;

- any pending suits or judgments;

- specific details of the condominium's insurance coverage;

- a current copy of the bylaws and rules and regulations;

- a statement that any improvements made either to the individual unit or to the limited common elements of the condominium assigned to the unit comply with the condominium declaration; and

- a statement of whether the condominium is located wholly or partially within a development subject to the Property Owners' Association Act.

The association may impose a charge of up to $100 for the preparation of the documents and certifications.

If the sale has not closed within 60 days from the date that the documents were provided to the buyer, the buyer may request written confirmation that the information has not changed. If the confirmation is not provided, or if there have been material changes, the purchaser may void the contract.

In Practice . . .

Condominium resale contracts must include wording to the effect that: (1) the offer is contingent on receipt of the condo documents; (2) the condo documents must be received by the purchaser within 15 days after the date of contract acceptance; and (3) the purchaser has three days in which to rescind the contract after receiving the documents.

TIME-SHARE OWNERSHIP

There are two types of time-share ownership recognized by the Virginia Time-Share Act [§55-360 et seq.]:

1. *Time-share estate* means a right to occupy a unit (or any of several units) during five or more separated time periods over a period of at least five years. The time-share estate includes renewal options, coupled with either a freehold interest or an estate for years (that is, a lease) in all or part of a time-share project.

2. *Time-share use* means a right to occupy a time-share unit or any of several time-share units during five or more separated time periods over a period of at least five years, including renewal options, *not coupled with* a freehold estate or an estate for years in a time-share project. Time-share use does not mean a right subject to a first-come, first-served, space-available basis, such as exists in a country club, motel or health spa.

The REB is charged with the administrative responsibility for the Time-Share Act.

Creation of a Time-Share

The developer of a time-share project must file and record with the REB a time-share *project instrument* that defines the project being created. This process establishes a time-share association in accordance with the Virginia Nonstock Corporations Act [§13.1-801].

A time-share association must be set up before any time-share estates may be sold. The project must be named, and the name must include the words *time-share, time-share interest, interval ownership, vacation ownership* or other terms recognized in the industry.

Items that are to be included in the project instrument include:

- the name of the time-share project;

- the complete address and legal description of the project;

- a description of the property;

- identification of the time periods;

- identification of the time-shares and the method by which additional time-shares may be created;

- the method used to allocate common expenses and voting rights assigned to each time-share;

- restrictions on use, occupancy, alteration or alienation;

- the method by which the managing entity will provide maintenance of the time-share, if maintenance is to be provided; and

- provisions for amending the time-share instrument.

Public Offering Statement

The POS filed for a time-share project is similar to the POS filed for a condominium. The developer may not convey any interest or advertise the property until the POS has been approved. If the time-share is being converted from another type of ownership, additional information is required regarding repairs made during the preceding three years and the physical condition of the structure. The purpose and value of reserve funds must be disclosed.

If the property to be converted is currently leased, tenants must be given 90 days' notice of the intent to convert the property to a time-share project. The tenants then have 60 days in which to contract with the developer to purchase the unit currently occupied if that unit is to be part of the overall project. Tenants on month-to-month leases must be given 120 days' notice to vacate.

Right to Rescind

The purchaser of a time-share interest at the project's *initial sale* has seven days to rescind the contract without penalty. The rescission period commences on the date of contract ratification or the receipt date of the POS, whichever is later. The right of rescission is statutory and cannot be waived.

Deposits

Money received by the developer as earnest money deposits or down payments must be placed in an escrow account established by the developer and held there through the rescission period. The developer also must post a surety bond with the REB in the amount of $25,000, or the amount of the deposits received, whichever is greater. If any purchaser exercises the statutory right of rescission, the developer has 45 days in which to refund all monies paid by the purchaser.

Advertisements

Advertisements used for the marketing of time-share interests that offer gifts or prizes must clearly disclose the retail value of the gift or prize offered. The ad must also disclose the terms and conditions under which the gift is offered; the odds of actually winning a prize; and the number of gifts or prizes to be awarded. The ad must include the offer's expiration date and a statement that the offer is made for the

purpose of soliciting the purchase of a time-share estate.

Transfer of Control

The developer remains in control of the project until 90 percent of the time-share estate has been sold or when all amenities and facilities have been completed, whichever is later. This is referred to as the *developer control period*. The developer control period may not exceed ten years after the sale of the first time-share interest. At the conclusion of the developer control period, the time-share owners' association assumes control and responsibility for the management and maintenance of the project. The developer must transfer control of the project to the owners' association without charging any fee. The owners' association may appoint or elect a managing agent for the project.

The owners' association has a statutory lien on every time-share estate in the project for unpaid regular and special assessments.

Beginning in the second year of owners' association management of the time-share project, the association must file an annual report with all owners. The report includes financial statements of the association, a list of officers and/or directors and projected assessments for the coming year. The bylaws of the association may be changed by a vote of the owners. Should the owners decide to terminate the time-share project, approval by 51 percent of the voting interest of the association is required.

Resale of Time-Share

A *resale* of a time-share interest by any person other than the developer is subject to rules similar to those governing the resale of a condominium. The seller must obtain a *Certificate of Resale* from the owners' association. The certificate contains a copy of the time-share instruments; current financial statements; current bylaws; current rules and regulations of the association; fees and assessments; a disclosure of any liens that may be pending on the time-share for nonpayment of fees; and a statement of pending litigation against the developer, owners' association or managing entity relative to the time-share project. The association may charge up to $50 for the certificate of resale.

The buyer in a time-share resale has the right to rescind the contract within five days following receipt of the certificate of resale or actual transfer, whichever occurs first. This right is without penalty and may be for any reason. Once the contract has closed, however, all rights of rescission are waived.

Statute of Limitations

Any action for misrepresentation of information in the project instruments, the POS or any contract must be initiated within two years of the date of the contract.

VIRGINIA PROPERTY OWNERS' ASSOCIATION ACT

The Virginia Property Owners' Association Act (POA) permits certain noncondominium property owners to form associations similar to condominium associations. [§55-508] The act recognizes that within neighborhoods or developments there are common areas that benefit all owners. For a fee, the association may provide for the upkeep and maintenance of such areas. The association may also impose certain restrictions on the member property owners.

Exemptions

Condominiums, cooperatives, time-share estates and campgrounds are exempt from the Act because these properties only exist under the conditions permitted by the act. However, if one of these types of ownership is located within an area that has been declared to be under the POA,

the property is subject to both sets of regulations.

Disclosure Requirements

Any party who sells property subject to the act must include a statement *in the sales contract* to the effect that

- the property is located in a development that is subject to the POA Act;

- the act requires the seller to obtain a disclosure packet from the POA and to provide that packet to the buyer;

- the buyer may cancel the contract within three days after receiving the packet or being advised that the packet will not be provided; and

- the rights to rescind the contract are waived if those rights are not exercised prior to closing.

If the contract does not contain these disclosures, the sole remedy for the buyer is to rescind the contract prior to closing.

POA Disclosure Packet

The information to be disclosed in the POA packet is essentially the same information included in condominium documents, although a survey is included. The information in the packet must be current within 30 days of contract ratification.

The association is required to make the packet available within 14 days after an owner/member (or an owner/member's authorized agent) files a written request. The association may charge up to $100 for providing the information. The associations's failure to deliver the packet in a timely manner waives any claim for delinquent assessments or fines. The maximum liability to the association for failing to provide the packet in a timely manner is actual damages, not to exceed $500.

Purchaser's Right to Rescind

The purchaser has the right to rescind the contract

- within three days after the date of the contract, if the packet or notice that the packet is unavailable was provided first, *or*

- within three days after receiving the packet or notice that the packet is not available (if the packet or notice is hand-delivered), *or*
- within six days after the postmark date of either the packet or the notice if the information was sent by U.S. mail.

If the purchaser elects to rescind, the notice of rescission must be hand-delivered or sent by U.S. mail (return receipt requested) to the owner. Rescission is without penalty, and the purchaser is entitled to a full refund of any earnest money given. Any rights to rescind the contract must be exercised prior to closing.

Questions

1. *B*, *J* and *E* own a parcel of property as tenants in common. *E* sells the entire parcel to *D*. Which of the following is true of this situation?

   a. *D* is now a tenant in common with *B* and *J*.
   b. *D* owns the parcel in severalty.
   c. *B* or *J* can void the contract, but *E* is bound.
   d. The contract is void, no one is bound and nothing conveys.

2. How is a joint tenancy created in Virginia?

   a. By an act of the parties
   b. By operation of law
   c. By dissolution of a tenancy in common
   d. All of the above

3. *S* and *J* own property as joint tenants. *S* dies intestate with no surviving children. What does *S*'s spouse receive?

   a. A one-third fee simple interest by virtue of dower or curtesy rights.
   b. *S*'s entire share.
   c. Nothing.
   d. *S*'s spouse must renounce the will in order to receive the property.

4. *G* and *B* own real property as joint tenants with right of survivorship. *G* dies owing money to creditors. Which of the following is correct?

   a. *B* owns the property in severalty and is liable to the creditors.
   b. *B* owns the property and is not liable to the creditors.
   c. *B* owns the property except for a share owned by the creditors that represents the debts' percentage of the property value.
   d. *G*'s wife owns the property interest held by her husband and is liable for the debts incurred by her husband.

5. When a person wants to create a condominium, which of the following statements is correct?

   a. The structures on the property being declared a condominium must be at least two stories.
   b. A condominium regime can only be created on unimproved land.
   c. The word *condominium* must appear in the name of the property.
   d. A condominium regime can be created only for residential use.

6. *B* and *M* own land as tenants by the entirety. *B* signs a contract to sell his share of the property to *J*. Under these facts, all of the following are true *EXCEPT*:

   a. *B* cannot sell his half-interest.
   b. While the contract appears valid, *B* cannot perform.
   c. *J* could hold *B* answerable for his inability to perform under the contract.
   d. *M* is now the sole owner of the land.

7. Contracts for the initial purchase of a condominium may be rescinded without penalty how many days after the later of contract ratification or receipt of the POS?

    a. 5 days   c. 14 days
    b. 10 days   d. 21 days

8. Which of the following is necessary for a corporation to convey property by deed?

    a. Corporate seal
    b. Proper signatures of all corporate officers
    c. Corporate name and required number of signatures
    d. Notarization

9. *H* is the owner of a time-share unit, which he bought several years ago from the developer. On March 2, *H* accepts an offer from *J* to buy the unit. On March 4, *H* hand-delivers the certificate of resale to J. On April 12, *H* transfers ownership of the unit to *J*. If *J* should decide to rescind the contract, what is the latest date when *J* may do so without incurring a penalty?

    a. March 7   c. March 15
    b. March 9   d. April 17

10. If a condominium unit owner fails to pay the owners' association's assessment against his or her unit, the owners' association may:

    a. place a lien against the unit.
    b. garnish the owner's wages.
    c. nothing; as a stockholder, the unit owner has priority.
    d. revoke the unit owner's privileges and rights.

11. The party responsible for the management and maintenance of a project on behalf of an owners' association is referred to as the

    a. owners' association.
    b. managing agent.
    c. developer.
    d. property manager.

12. When the owner's interest in a time-share includes either a freehold interest or an estate for years, it is what type?

    a. Time-share use
    b. Time-share estate
    c. Time-share fee
    d. Time-share demise

13. What is the statute of limitations on any action for misrepresentation of information as it applies to time-shares?

    a. Seven years
    b. Two years
    c. One year
    d. No limitation

14. Which of the following is true regarding Virginia's community property laws?

    a. Since 1991, the Virginia statute is patterned after California's.
    b. Virginia recognizes only some community property provisions.
    c. Augmented estates are the same as community property provisions.
    d. Virginia is not a community property state.

5 Legal Descriptions

DESCRIBING REAL ESTATE

The most common method of describing real estate in Virginia is a combination of metes-and-bounds and lot-and-block.

Licensees should use great care in describing property. Both the real estate plat map and tax records, as well as at least one deed by which the land was conveyed in the past, should be checked to verify that the proper legal description is being used. The description should enable the parties — or a court — to determine exactly what land the parties intended to convey. *Parol evidence* (that is, evidence of facts and circumstances not included in the deed or contract) is admissible in a court proceeding if the facts were well known in the community at the time the deed was made.

METHODS OF DESCRIPTION

The description of land by any of the following methods is legally sufficient, if the county or city and state are included:

- By courses and distances with an identifiable starting point (metes-and-bounds method)

- As bounded by natural or artificial objects or by the land of named persons (monuments method)

- By reference to a recorded map, plat, survey, deed or other writing (lot-and-block method)

- By number or code on a recorded subdivision (subdivision method)

- By geodetic survey of townships, ranges, meridians, and so forth (rectangular government survey method)

- By house number and named street, where there is an established system of numbering

- By any name by which the land is generally known and identifiable

- As occupied or acquired by a named person at a definite time

- As being all the land of the grantor in a designated way or acquired in a specific way

---

FOR EXAMPLE . . .

Here is a common property description:

All those certain lots, pieces or parcels of land, situated in the city of Norfolk, Virginia, known, numbered and designated on the Plat of Estabrook Corp., made by S.W. Armistead, C.E., February 1920, and recorded in the clerk's office of the Circuit Court of the City of Chesapeake, Virginia, in Map Book 17, page 4, as Lots No. 35 and 36, located on the North side of Amherst Street in Block "E" in said Subdivision known as Estabrook, and appurtenances thereunto belonging said lots being 25 × 100 feet each.

A shortened form is frequently used in listing agreements and sales contracts:

> Lots 35 and 36, Block E, Plat of Estabrook, Norfolk, Virginia 23513, also known and described as 36 Amherst Street.

The following would also be an acceptable description:

> All that land known as Warrens Crossing, as purchased by Nicholas Lilly on June 17, 1984, and bounded on the north by Richmond Hwy., on the south by Muddy Run, on the east by the farm belonging to John Evans, and on the south by the Redly Estate owned by Elizabeth Davies.

False Descriptions

A false description does not invalidate the deed if, after rejecting the false description, enough remains to permit reliable identification of the land to be conveyed. A complete description can be found in the deed that conveyed the property to the seller. The identical description should be used to convey the land to the buyer.

Settlement of Disputes

Disputed boundaries between two adjoining lands may be settled by express agreement. Virginia law provides for a court proceeding to establish boundaries.

In conflicts concerning true boundaries, Virginia law gives preference to methods of description in the following order:

1. Natural monuments or landmarks

2. Artificial monuments and established lines

3. Adjacent boundaries or lines of adjoining tracts

4. Calls for courses and distances

5. Designation of quantity, such as "approximately 3.5 acres"

This preference will not be applied where it would frustrate the intent of the parties.

In disputes among purchasers of lots shown on a plat, the metes and bounds established by accurate survey and corresponding calls of courses and distances noted on the plat will supersede errors in the plat and will control the dimensions and configuration of the lots.

SURVEYING AND SURVEYS

To engage in the practice of land surveying in Virginia, a person must hold a valid surveyor's license, unless exempted by the statute. Lenders are not allowed to require that a particular surveyor perform the survey in connection with making a loan to purchase real property. Surveys are recorded in the clerk's office of the circuit court where the land is located.

Four Types of Surveys

There are four types of surveys commonly used in Virginia:

1. A *subdivision plat* is a map of each parcel of land. The plat shows the subdivided lots, streets and similar features. The plat is generally created from a tract of land to subdivide it. The subdivided lots may or may not be "staked on the ground" once the plat has been created.

2. A *boundary survey*, as opposed to a subdivision plat, shows the boundary or perimeter of the parcel as taken from and applied to the ground. Corner stakes or other physical landmarks appear.

3. A *house location survey* is a boundary survey with the location of the house shown.

4. A *physical* or *as-built survey* is a house location survey with all other physical features of the subject property shown, including water courses, utility lines, fence lines, outbuildings and similar features.

A recently recorded survey of a subject property may reveal matters not shown in the record.

The attorney is primarily the person obligated to examine the survey. The real estate licensee, however, also should examine it. The licensee should be alert for the following "red flag" conditions. If any of these conditions exist, they should immediately be brought to the attention of an attorney as potential problem areas:

-   property boundaries that do not conform with the recorded plat;

-   structural encroachments by the property onto neighboring properties, or by neighboring structures onto the subject property;

-   fences that are not on the boundary line;

-   party walls;

-   riparian rights of others in streams, lakes and other bodies of water;

-   utilities that service other properties;

-   old roadways;

-   cemeteries;

-   violation of setback, side or rear building lines; and

-   property that may be landlocked.

Any defect shown on the survey should be reported and corrective action taken where necessary.

Plat Maps

In areas of Virginia where recorded plat maps are used in lieu of individual surveys, the appropriate lot must be identified and lot dimensions must be legibly shown. Necessary endorsements to the title insurance policy must be issued pertaining to easements, deed restrictions and property identification. The closing lawyer is responsible for obtaining the endorsements.

Subdivision Plat

In Virginia, a subdivision plat must contain all the necessary approvals of county or city officials. In addition the dedications or consents of all owners, trustees and other similar parties must be properly recorded. The law provides that the mere recordation of a plat transfers the streets, alleys and other areas set aside for public use to the county or municipality in fee simple.

Questions

1. All of the following are satisfactory legal descriptions *EXCEPT:*

    a. Lot 7, Block D, Plat of Red Valley
    b. The entire 77.5 Acres purchased by Edna Kelly on June 20, 1981, and known as Seaside Neck, Roanoke
    c. 727 Olean Drive, Fletcherton, Virginia
    d. Proceeding 120 feet due west of the intersection of the east line of J Street and the north line of 11th street to a point; thence north 10 degrees 31 minutes west 100 feet

2. A deed contains the following description:

    Lots 7 and 8, Block F, Section 3, Plat of Greydon, otherwise known as 14 Havers Drive, Venus, Virginia.

    In fact, Block F has only 6 lots, and the street address is Lot 5. Is this deed valid?

    a. No; a false element in a description invalidates the deed.
    b. No; because the lot description is faulty, a new deed is needed.
    c. Yes, if the buyer knows which property is meant.
    d. Yes; enough correct information remains to permit identification.

3. J and B bought neighboring lots in a new subdivision. The representation of the lots on the plat shows that B's land reaches to a creek and J's land falls just short of the creek. At the closing, a survey of the lots shows J with access to the creek, and leaves B without access. Who prevails regarding access to the creek?

    a. B; the original pictorial representation governs.
    b. B, because otherwise the developer is guilty of misrepresentation.
    c. J; the survey supersedes pictorial errors in the plat.
    d. A new survey must be drawn giving both buyers creek access.

4. A lender uses the services of only one licensed surveyor and will not accept other surveyors' surveys. Is this practice legal?

    a. Yes, provided the lender pays the cost of the survey.
    b. Yes, as long as the surveyor holds a valid license.
    c. No; surveyors are selected by the clerk's office of the circuit court where the land is located.
    d. No; the lender cannot require that a particular surveyor conduct the survey.

TAX LIENS

Uniform Taxation

In Virginia, real estate taxes are levied according to the proportion designated by tax laws. The Virginia Constitution requires that taxation be *uniform*. Uniform taxation requires that both the tax rate and the mode of assessing the taxable value must be uniformly applied to similar properties. That is, all property of the same class must be taxed alike.

However, the principle of uniformity does not prevent differences in taxation or the classification for taxation purposes of properties according to use in a business, trade or occupation.

Exemptions

Burial grounds and cemetery lots owned by a cemetery company or by lot owners and used exclusively for burial purposes are exempt from taxation.

The Virginia Constitution exempts property owned and exclusively occupied or used by religious organizations for worship purposes or ministerial residences. The exemption applies to both real and personal property.

Property owned by public libraries or nonprofit educational institutions is exempt, as long as it is primarily used for literary, scientific or educational purposes.

In addition, property used by its owner for religious, charitable, patriotic, historical, benevolent, cultural or public park and playground purposes is also exempt.

The controlling factor in determining whether private property is exempt from taxation is the *use* of the property. Public property, however, may be exempted from taxation without regard to its use.

Assessment

Taxes run with the land. The buyer of a property is responsible for paying real estate taxes for the current tax year from the date of purchase until the end of the year. In Virginia, the buyer is said to own the property on the date of settlement. Taxes should be prorated between the vendee and vendor as of the date of the sale. Any delinquent taxes should be paid by the vendor at closing. Penalties and interest on delinquent taxes are established by statute.

> *IN PRACTICE . . .*
> Unpaid taxes are a lien on real property. The settlement agent must verify that prior years' taxes have been paid, and ascertain the status of the current year's taxes. Any other information should be obtained from city or county tax offices.

Taxes are generally not payable in advance of the due date. However, each city and county has its own particular manner of assessing taxes and setting the due date. Real estate licensees should be aware of four phases of taxes:

1. Past-due taxes

2. Taxes currently due and payable

3. Taxes not yet due

4. Prepaid taxes

The taxes for the first two phases will be collected from the seller's proceeds and paid to the proper authority by the settlement attorney. In the third and fourth phases, there are no taxes to be paid at the time a sale is closed. The closer will prorate the taxes between buyer and seller.

In phase three, the seller will be charged with the portion of the taxes that represents the number of days he or she occupied the property. The buyer will be credited with the same amount.

In phase four, where the taxes have been prepaid, the seller will receive a credit for the amount of taxes already paid for the period of time that he or she will not be occupying the property. The buyer will be charged with the same amount.

Estimating Taxes

Sometimes, past-year taxes cannot be used to estimate current taxes. It is up to the real estate licensee to use whatever information is available to reasonably estimate the current year's taxes.

New Construction

In the case of new construction, the taxes on the land are prorated based on taxes for the past year. Taxes on the new improvements are estimated using the purchase price multiplied by the county or city assessment rate. Taxes are estimated from the date the certificate of occupancy is issued, or a partial assessment may be levied against new construction not yet completed. If the closing is significantly later than the date of the certificate of occupancy or the closing date

in the sales contract, the licensee should check to see if the property has been reassessed with the improvements.

Leases

As a general rule, the landlord under any ordinary lease is responsible for the taxes on the property; however, this does not apply to a perpetual leaseholder who is, in effect, the rightful owner of the property and is entitled to its use forever. In such a case, the burden of taxation is placed on the lessee. In the case of net leases, the tenant is usually responsible for payment of the taxes.

Tax Liens

Delinquent real property taxes are both a personal debt and a lien against the property. A tax lien on real property has priority over all other liens except court costs. Thus, a tax lien overrides a vendor's lien, even though the vendor's lien may have been first. A tax lien is also prior to the landlord's lien for rent.

The Virginia statutes give real estate taxes priority over a deed of trust in the distribution of proceeds under a foreclosure sale. The foreclosing trustee must satisfy all outstanding tax deficiencies before distributing the remaining proceeds to other creditors. If the statute's requirements are not complied with, delinquent taxes remain a debt against the purchaser at the sale.

A lien in favor of the United States for unpaid taxes, interest and penalties may arise against all real and personal property belonging to a taxpayer. The lien is perfected under Virginia law by filing notice of tax lien in the circuit court for the jurisdiction in which the taxpayer resides. The tax lien remains in effect until the taxes are paid.

When taxes on real estate in a county, city or town are delinquent on December 31 following the third anniversary of the date on which the taxes became due, the real estate may be sold to collect the tax.

FOR EXAMPLE . . .

C's property tax was due on June 10, 1996. *C* failed to pay. If the tax is still delinquent on December 31, 1999, *C*'s property may be sold for taxes on January 1, 2000.

At least 30 days before taking any action to sell the property, the tax-collecting officer must send a notice to the last known address of the property owner. Notice of the sale must be published in a newspaper of general circulation in the area 30 to 60 days prior to the commencement of the sale proceedings.

The sale proceedings are initiated by filing a suit in the circuit court of the county or city where the real estate is located. The owner of the real estate (or their heirs, successors and assigns) have the right to redeem the real estate *prior to the sale date* by paying all taxes, penalties and interest due, plus costs, including the cost of publication and a reasonable attorney's fee set by the court. The former owner of any real estate sold for delinquent real estate taxes is entitled to any receipts from the sale in excess of the taxes, penalties, interest and costs.

Special Assessments

There is a distinction between special assessments and general tax levies for purposes of funding government services and operations. *Special assessments* are taxes levied against specific benefitted properties to pay for limited local improvements. They are founded on the theory of benefits brought about by improvements to adjacent properties. This public improvement enhances the value of a specific property — a sidewalk, for instance, or a re-paved alley. A special assessment is distinguished from an improvement that benefits the entire community, such as a park.

The statute specifically provides that notice must be given to abutting landowners of the contemplated improvements before the ordinance authorizing the improvements is put into effect. This gives the landowner an opportunity to be heard concerning the adoption or rejection of such an ordinance. The statute provides for special assessments relating to sewers, street paving and other local public improvements.

The only properties subject to special assessments are those of abutting landowners.

Local improvements may be ordered by a town or city council (with costs to be defrayed by special assessment) following receipt of a petition from not less than three-fourths of the landowners who will be affected by the assessment. However, the council may issue such an improvement order without a petition.

The amount of special assessment for a local improvement constitutes a lien on the property benefited by the improvement, enforceable by a suit in court. Property owners have the right to appear before the municipal authorities and protest both the authorization of the improvements and the assessments.

LIENS OTHER THAN TAXES

Mechanic's Liens

Anyone who performs labor or furnishes material with a value of $50 or more for the construction, removal, repair or improvement of any structure has a right of lien on both the land and the building. The object of the law is to give laborers and materialmen the security of a lien on the property to the extent that they have added to its value.

The Virginia Mechanics' Lien Disclosure Act [§11-2.4] requires that the seller of property disclose in the sales contract a warning that an effective mechanic's lien may be filed against the real property even after settlement.

The Act's purpose is to protect contractors, brokers, purchasers, title agents and insurers from builders or owners who contracted for improvements, sold the property and never paid the contractor. The Act requires that each residential sales contract include the following:

NOTICE

Virginia law §43-1 et seq. permits persons who have performed labor or furnished materials for the construction, removal, repair or improvement of any building or structure to file a lien against the property. This lien may be filed at any time after the work is commenced or the material is furnished, but not later than the earlier of (i) 90 days from the last day of the month in which the lienor last performed work or furnished materials or (ii) 90 days from the time the construction, removal, repair or improvement is terminated.

AN EFFECTIVE LIEN FOR WORK PERFORMED, PRIOR TO THE DATE OF SETTLEMENT, MAY BE FILED AFTER SETTLEMENT. LEGAL COUNSEL SHOULD BE CONSULTED.

While inclusion of the statement is mandatory, failure to include it will not void the contract.

A general contractor or a subcontractor may perfect a mechanic's lien by filing a memorandum of mechanic's lien and an affidavit with the clerk of court in the jurisdiction in which the property or structure is located. The filing must be within 90 days of the last day of the month in which the contractor last performed labor or furnished materials. However, under no circumstances may filing occur later than 90 days from the time the building is completed or the work otherwise terminated.

Written notice must be given to the owner of the property. The notice memorandum generally contains

- the name of the owner of the property;

- the name of the claimant;

- the amount of the claim;

- the time when the amount is or will be due and payable; and

- a brief description of the property.

A mechanic's lien is enforced by a suit filed within six months of recording the memorandum of lien or 60 days from the completion or termination of work on the structure, whichever is later. If the person who ordered the work owns less than the fee simple estate in the land, only his or her actual interest is subject to the lien.

When a buyer constructs a building or other structure, or undertakes repairs to an existing building or structure before the transaction has closed, the owner's interest will be subject to any mechanic's lien if the owner knows about the activity.

When a lien (such as a deed of trust) is created on land before work is begun or materials furnished, the deed of trust is a first lien on the land and a second lien on the building or structure. A deed of trust that is recorded before the work began is entitled to priority to the extent of the estimated value of the property *without the improvements for which the lien is claimed.*

Typically, the seller must execute an affidavit at closing that declares no work has been performed or any materials furnished within 120 days before the date of closing. This declaration ensures that no mechanic can file a lien against the property after closing for labor performed or materials furnished prior to closing. Nonetheless, a buyer should be advised to obtain additional assurances that no mechanic's liens can be filed.

Closing agents are charged with the responsibility to advise buyers of possible mechanic's lien filings and must inform buyers about title insurance protection.

A lien waiver should be demanded for new construction stating that all amounts have been paid for labor performed and materials furnished in connection with the construction. The waiver should be executed by the general contractor and all subcontractors. However, no waiver is required if affirmative mechanic's lien coverage is provided by a title insurance company.

Judgments

Every money judgment rendered in Virginia by any court, or by confession of judgment, constitutes a lien on any real estate the judgment debtor owns or may own in the future. The lien is effective from the date the judgment is docketed (that is, indexed by the clerk of court). It is prudent to docket the judgment in the city or county in which the debtor's property is located. If the debtor currently has no property, it is wise to docket the judgment wherever property is located that may become the debtor's in the future (for instance, property owned by family members).

A writ of execution may be issued and the judgment enforced within 20 years from the date the judgment was rendered. A judgment may be extended beyond its 20-year life by a motion made in the circuit court, following notice to the judgment debtor and redocketing of the judgment.

If the real estate is conveyed to a grantee for value subject to a judgment lien, the judgment creditor must bring the suit to enforce the judgment lien within ten years from the date the grantee's deed was recorded.

If the judgment is for recovery of specific real property, a *writ of possession* is needed. If the judgment debtor owns real estate outside Virginia, the debtor may be required to convey it to a sheriff.

Within 30 days of the satisfaction (that is, payment) of a judgment, a judgment creditor must release the judgment wherever it is docketed. Failure to do so within ten days of demand by the judgment debtor makes the creditor subject to a fine.

Estate and Inheritance Tax Liens

A lien arises on all property, real and personal, of every decedent who has a taxable estate located in the Commonwealth of Virginia if the decedent's estate fails to pay the tax imposed by the Virginia Estate Tax Act.

In the case of a nonresident decedent who has a taxable estate in Virginia, the lien arises automatically at the time of the nonresident's death. In the case of a resident decedent, the liens attach to the real estate only when a memorandum is filed by the department of taxation in the clerk's office of the county or city where such real estate is located. Once it attaches, the lien is enforceable for ten years from the date of the decedent's death.

In Virginia, the tax imposed is a *succession tax* rather than an estate tax: a tax on the right to succeed to the property or an interest in it, not the right to transmit it. The tax is not levied on the property of which an estate is composed, but on the shifting of economic benefits and the privilege of receiving such benefits.

Attachments

The mere issuance of an attachment creates no lien on the real estate. To create a lien, it is necessary for the officer to show that levy (actual attachment or seizure) was made.

Lis Pendens

A *lis pendens,* or pending suit, does not bind or affect a subsequent purchaser of real estate unless a memorandum is properly recorded giving notice of the suit. The memorandum of notice states the title of the suit, its general object and the court in which it is pending. The notice declares the amount of the claim, describes the property and names the person whose estate is intended to be affected.

If the lis pendens is not docketed as provided by the statutes, a purchaser without notice of the pending suit takes good title, with no lien on the land by virtue of the pending suit.

Vendor's Lien

In Virginia, if any person conveys any real estate and the purchase money remains unpaid at the time of the conveyance, the vendor will not have a lien for the unpaid purchase money unless the lien is expressly reserved on the face of the deed. The object of this statute is to make the lien a matter of record, putting all persons who deal with the property on notice of all liens and encumbrances. The extent of the vendor's lien does not depend on the extent of the vendor's interest in the land conveyed but on the contract of the parties as gathered from the deed itself.

Landlord's Lien

The Virginia statutes give a landlord a right of lien. It exists independently of the right to hold property for payment of rent. When the landlord's lien for rent is obtained, it relates back to the very beginning of the tenancy and takes precedence over any lien that any other person has obtained or created against goods (personal property) on the leased premises since the tenancy began. A lien legally attaches to all property on the premises when it is asserted or on the premises within 30 days prior to attachment of lien. The landlord can seize the tenant's goods only to the extent necessary to satisfy the rent justly believed to be due.

Commercial Broker's Lien

A commercial real estate broker has a lien on the rent paid by the tenant in the amount of the compensation (commission) agreed on by the owner and the broker.

Questions

1. Which of the following is true of uniform real estate taxation in Virginia?

   a. Tax rates and assessments must be uniformly applied to similar properties.
   b. All properties pay the same amount of tax.
   c. Only the tax rate needs to be uniform.
   d. Uniformity is a common law principle.

2. *B*'s house is near the end of a block; right beside her house on the corner lot is *H*'s Bakery. How must these properties be treated for real estate tax purposes?

   a. There can be no difference between them.
   b. They will be classified differently, according to use.
   c. A sliding value scale may be applied to businesses but not to residences, which are strictly ad valorem.
   d. Because the bakery abuts a residential zone, it must be treated as a residence.

3. All of the following types of real property are exempt from real property taxation *EXCEPT:*

   a. burial grounds.
   b. government-owned land.
   c. land owned by nonprofit educational institutions.
   d. land owned by handicapped persons.

4. Which of the following statements is true regarding taxes on new construction?

   a. Taxes are estimated using the purchase price multiplied by the state assessment rate.
   b. Taxes are estimated from the date of the certificate of occupancy.
   c. Improvements are not assessed as part of the previously existing property.
   d. The statutory appreciation rate is applied to new construction to estimate the current year's fair market value.

5. In Virginia, who owns a property (for real estate tax purposes) on the date of sale?

   a. The buyer owns it.
   b. The seller owns it.
   c. It is divided evenly, with each party paying half of the tax for that day.
   d. This item must be negotiated.

6. When real property is sold to satisfy a real estate tax lien, the buyer at the tax sale receives a

   a. certificate of sale.
   b. deed.
   c. cloud on title.
   d. certificate of equitable title.

7. *J* is relieved to learn that her home will soon be served by a city sewer line. How will this improvement most likely be paid for?

   a. General real estate tax
   b. Municipal bonds
   c. Special assessment
   d. State road-use tax

8. How long after the work was done may a mechanic wait before filing a mechanic's lien?

    a. No more than 30 days
    b. No more than 60 days
    c. No more than 90 days
    d. No more than 6 months

9. How soon after filing the lien must the mechanic enforce it by filing suit?

    a. Within three months
    b. Within six months
    c. Within nine months
    d. Within one year

10. Within what period of time must a creditor on a judgment enforce the judgment once it is rendered?

    a. Within 6 months
    b. Within 1 year
    c. Within 5 years
    d. Within 20 years

THE CONTRACT

The actual contract used for the purchase and sale of real property may take any form. The only requirement is that it be in enough detail to clearly state the agreement between the parties.

Local real estate associations often have standard forms to be used by their members (for an example, see Figure 7.1).

It is customary for real estate licensees to assist buyers and sellers with the preparation of the contract by filling in the blanks on the form. *As with all legal matters, real estate brokers and salespersons should refrain from trying to explain the legal technicalities.* Improper or misunderstood explanations could subject the licensee to legal action later.

> **IN PRACTICE . . .**
> As with the listing agreement form, all blanks should be filled in. If the item does not apply, the notation "N/A" ("Not Applicable") should be inserted.

STATUTE OF FRAUDS

Virginia's Statute of Frauds prevents the enforcement of an oral contract or promise. [§11.1] The statute does not invalidate oral contracts; rather, it addresses the contract's enforceability. The statute bars any action concerning a contract for the sale of real estate or for a lease on real property *for more than one year* unless the document is in writing.

Although an oral lease for a term of more than one year is unenforceable and the parties cannot be compelled to perform, they are nonetheless free to make and comply with such an agreement.

CONTRACT PROCEDURES

Use of a standard form does not excuse the licensee from pointing out to both parties that the contract is a legally binding document and that legal advice should be sought if either party has legal questions. The parties may make the agreement contingent on review and approval by an attorney.

Power of Attorney

Sometimes, a party cannot be present at the closing and must be represented by an attorney-in-fact. In Virginia, the power of attorney must specify the transaction and the parties involved: a general power of attorney will not suffice. The power of attorney must be notarized and recorded with the deed.

> **IN PRACTICE . . .**
> Many military notaries are from outside Virginia and may not comply with the requirements of the Virginia Code.

Figure 7.1   Regional Sales Contract and Virginia Addendum

REGINAL SALES CONTRACT

This SALES CONTRACT ("Contract") is made on _____, 19____, ("Contract Date")
between_____ ("Purchaser")
and _____ ("Seller") who
hereby confirm and acknowledge by their initials and signatures below the prior disclosure that in this real estate transaction _____
_____ ("Listing Company") represents
the Seller, and _____ ("Selling Company") represents
☐ the Purchaser OR ☐ the Seller. The Listing Company and Selling Company are collectively referred to as ("Broker"). (If the brokerage firm is acting as a dual representative for both the Seller and the Purchaser, then the appropriate disclosure form is attached to and made a part of this Contract.)

1. **REAL PROPERTY.** The Purchaser shall buy and the Seller shall sell for the sales price ("Sales Price"), the Seller's entire interest in the land (with all improvements, rights and appurtenances) described as follows: TAX Map/ID # _____,
Legal Description: Lot(s)_____, Block/Square _____, Section _____,
Subdivision or Condominium _____, Unit # _____, Parking Space(s) # _____,
County/City _____. Deed Book/Liber _____, Page/Folio # _____,
Street Address: _____, State _____, Zip Code _____, ("Property").

2. **PERSONAL PROPERTY, FIXTURES AND UTILITIES.** The Sales Price includes the following personal property and fixtures: A. Any existing built-in heating and central air conditioning equipment, plumbing and lighting fixtures, sump pump, attic fans, storm windows, storm doors, screens, installed wall-to-wall carpeting, window shades, blinds, smoke and heat detectors, tv antennas, exterior trees and shrubs and, B. The items marked YES below as currently installed or offered.

YES NO		YES NO		YES NO		YES NO	
☐ ☐	Stove or Range	☐ ☐	Disposer	☐ ☐	Ceiling Fan(s) # ____	☐ ☐	Alarm System
☐ ☐	Cooktop	☐ ☐	Freezer	☐ ☐	Washer	☐ ☐	Intercom
☐ ☐	Wall Oven(s) # ____	☐ ☐	Window Fan(s) # ____	☐ ☐	Dryer	☐ ☐	Storage Shed(s) # ____
☐ ☐	Refrigerator(s) # ____	☐ ☐	Window A/C Unit(s) # ____	☐ ☐	Furnace Humidifier	☐ ☐	Garage Opener(s)# ____
☐ ☐	w/ Ice maker	☐ ☐	Pool, Equip. & Cover	☐ ☐	Electronic Air Filter	☐ ☐	w/ remote(s) #____
☐ ☐	Dishwasher	☐ ☐	Hot Tub, Equip. & Cover	☐ ☐	Central Vacuum	☐ ☐	Playground Equipment
☐ ☐	Built-in Microwave	☐ ☐	Satellite Dish and Equip.	☐ ☐	Water Treatment System	☐ ☐	Wood Stove
☐ ☐	Trash Compactor	☐ ☐	Window Treatments	☐ ☐	Exhaust Fan(s)	☐ ☐	Fireplace Screen/ Doors

Other: _____
_____

WATER, SEWAGE, HEATING AND CENTRAL AIR CONDITIONING: (Check all that apply)
Water Supply: ☐Public ☐ Well _____   Hot Water: ☐ Oil ☐ Gas ☐ Elec. ☐ Other _____
Sewage Disposal: ☐Public ☐ Septic # BR _____   Air Conditioning: ☐ Oil ☐ Gas ☐ Elec. ☐ Heat Pump ☐ Other _____
                                                    Heating: ☐ Oil ☐ Gas ☐ Elec. ☐ Heat Pump ☐ Other _____

3. **EQUIPMENT, MAINTENANCE AND CONDITION.** The Purchaser accepts the Property in "AS IS" condition as of the Contract Date except as otherwise provided herein. The Seller warrants that the existing appliances, heating, cooling, plumbing, electrical and mechanical systems and equipment and smoke and heat detectors (as required) shall be in normal working order as of the possession date. The Seller shall deliver the Property in substantially the same condition as on the Contract Date and in broom clean condition with all trash and debris removed. The Purchaser and the Seller shall not hold the Broker liable for any breach of this paragraph.

4. **PRICE AND FINANCING**
   A. Down Payment $ _____

   B. Financing   1. First Trust $ _____

                   2. Second Trust - addendum attached $ _____

                   3. Trust (Seller Financing) - addendum attached $ _____

                   TOTAL FINANCING $ _____

                   TOTAL SALES PRICE OF THE PROPERTY $ _____

Figure 7.1   *(continued).*

5. DEPOSIT. A. The Purchaser has made a deposit ("Deposit") with _____ ("Escrow Agent") of
□ $ _____ by check and/or □ $ _____ by note due and payable on _____ , 19 ___ , receipt of
which is hereby acknowledged. B. The Deposit shall be placed in an escrow account of the Escrow Agent after the Contract Acceptance to conform
with the laws and regulations of the appropriate jurisdiction and/or, if VA financing applies, as required by Title 38 of the U.S. Code. This account may
be interest bearing and all parties waive any claim to interest resulting from the Deposit. The Deposit shall be held in escrow until: i. Credited toward the
Sales Price at settlement; ii. All parties have agreed in writing as to its disposition; iii. A court of competent jurisdiction orders disbursement and all appeal
periods have expired; or, iv. Disposed of in any other manner authorized by the laws and regulations of the appropriate jurisdiction.

6. DOWN PAYMENT. The balance of the down payment shall be paid at settlement by certified or cashier's check or by bank wired funds.

7. FIRST DEED OF TRUST. Purchaser shall □ OBTAIN OR □ ASSUME: a □ Conventional □ FHA □ VA □ Other _____
First Deed of Trust loan amortized over _____ years at a □ FIXED OR an □ ADJUSTABLE rate bearing (initial) interest of _____ %
per year or market rate available. Special Terms (if any): _____
_____

ASSUMPTION ONLY: Assumption fee, if any, and all charges related to the assumption shall be paid by the Purchaser. If the Purchaser assumes the
Seller's loan, A. The Purchaser and the Seller □ shall, OR □ shall not obtain a release of the Seller's liability to the U.S. Government for the repayment
of the loan by settlement.   B. The Purchaser and Seller □ shall, OR □ shall not obtain substitution of the Seller's VA entitlement by settlement.
C. Balances of any assumed loans, secondary financing and cash down payments are approximate.

8. ADDITIONAL FINANCING TERMS.
A. □ CONVENTIONAL FINANCING. If applicable, the Purchaser shall □ pay at settlement, OR □ finance any initial private mortgage insurance.
Based on the financing terms specified in this Contract, the Seller shall pay _____ toward the Purchaser's
normal settlement charges, (including but not limited to loan origination fees, discount fees, buy down or subsidy fees, prepaids or other settlement
charges as allowed by the lender). The Purchaser shall pay all remaining Purchaser's settlement charges. ~~If the lender's appraisal is not equal to or
greater than the Sales Price and the parties are unable to agree upon mutually acceptable terms, then it shall be the Seller's option to lower the Sales
Price to the appraised value and this Contract shall remain in full force and effect at the lower Sales Price. If the Seller does not exercise that option, it
is the Purchaser's option to proceed with the settlement at the Sales Price and Seller and Purchaser shall sign any appropriate amendment(s). Each
election must be made by Notice within 3 Days after Notice from the other party. If the parties fail to agree, this Contract shall become void and the
Deposit shall be refunded in full to the Purchaser according to the terms of the DEPOSIT paragraph.~~

B. □ VA OR □ FHA FINANCING
The Purchaser shall □ pay at settlement, OR □ finance any VA Funding Fee or FHA initial Mortgage Insurance Premium. Based on the financing
specified in this Contract, the Seller shall pay _____ toward the Purchaser's normal settlement charges (including
but not limited to loan origination fees, discount fees, buydown or subsidy fees, prepaids or other settlement charges as allowed by the lender) except
that the total amount of any lender charges which cannot by law or regulation be charged to the Purchaser shall first be deducted from this amount, and
the remaining balance, if any, shall then be applied to the Purchaser's other settlement charges. The Purchaser shall pay all remaining Purchaser's
settlement charges. If VA or FHA financing applies, it is expressly agreed that, notwithstanding any other provisions of this Contract, the Purchaser shall
not be obligated to complete the purchase of the Property described herein or to incur any penalty by forfeiture of earnest money deposits or otherwise
unless the Purchaser has been given in accordance with HUD/FHA or VA requirements a written statement by the Federal Housing Commissioner or
Direct Endorsement Lender/Department of Veterans Affairs or the Lender Approval Processing Program (LAPP) underwriter setting forth the appraised
value of the Property (excluding closing costs) of not less than $ _____ . The Purchaser shall have the privilege and option of proceeding with
consummation of the Contract without regard to the amount of the appraised valuation. THE APPRAISED VALUATION IS ARRIVED AT TO DETERMINE
THE MAXIMUM MORTGAGE THE DEPARTMENT OF HOUSING AND URBAN DEVELOPMENT /DEPARTMENT OF VETERANS AFFAIRS WILL
INSURE/GUARANTEE. HUD/DEPARTMENT OF VETERANS AFFAIRS AND THE MORTGAGEE DOES NOT WARRANT THE VALUE NOR THE
CONDITION OF THE PROPERTY. THE PURCHASER SHOULD SATISFY HIMSELF/HERSELF THAT THE PRICE AND CONDITION OF THE
PROPERTY ARE ACCEPTABLE.
If VA Financing applies, the Purchaser agrees that should the Purchaser elect to complete the purchase at an amount in excess of the reasonable
value established by the Department of Veterans Affairs, the Purchaser shall pay such excess amount in cash from a source which the Purchaser agrees
to disclose to the Department of Veterans Affairs, and which the Purchaser represents will not be borrowed funds except as approved by the Department
of Veterans Affairs. The Purchaser's exercise of the option shall be made in writing within 3 Days of the notification to the Purchaser of the appraised
value, or this Contract shall become void and the Deposit shall be refunded in full to the Purchaser according to the terms of the DEPOSIT paragraph.
If FHA financing applies, the Purchaser's exercise of the option of proceeding with consummation of the Contract without regard to the amount of
the appraised valuation shall be made in writing within 3 Days of the notification to the Purchaser of the appraised value, or this Contract shall become
void and the Deposit shall be refunded in full to the Purchaser according to the terms of the DEPOSIT paragraph. The FHA loan amount is approximate
because the financed acquisition costs cannot be determined until the time of settlement.

9. FINANCING CONTINGENCY. If the **PRICE AND FINANCING** paragraph above includes financing, the terms of this paragraph shall apply.
The Purchaser shall make written loan application, if applicable, within 7 Days following the Contract Acceptance. The Purchaser grants permission for
the Selling Company and the lender to disclose to the Listing Company and the Seller general information available about the progress of the loan
application and loan approval process. The Purchaser may obtain alternative financing for which the Purchaser is qualified provided there is no additional
expense to the Seller and the settlement date is not delayed.
A. This Contract is contingent on the Purchaser securing a firm, written commitment for the financing specified in this Contract, or lender's approval
of assumption, if required ("Specified Financing"). The Purchaser shall furnish written evidence of the lender's commitment or approval to the Seller within
_____ Days of Contract Acceptance, which commitment or approval the Purchaser agrees to pursue diligently.
   i.   If the Purchaser is unable to obtain the Specified Financing during this contingency period, the Purchaser may unilaterally extend the
        contingency period for 15 Days by giving the Seller:
        a. A Notice of Purchaser's intention to do so, together with;
        b. Written evidence from the lender showing that all information in the lender's possession indicates that the Purchaser's loan should be
            approved.
   ii. After the expiration of the contingency period (including the 15 Day unilateral extension, if applicable), but prior to Delivery of lender's written
        commitment, the Seller may with Notice to the Purchaser:
        a. ~~Declare this Contract void, OR;~~
        b. Elect to provide the Specified Financing to the Purchaser at any time prior to Delivery of lender's written commitment.
   iii. The Purchaser shall have the right to Deliver to the Seller a copy of a written letter of rejection for the Specified Financing from the lender
        along with a written request for release from the Contract.
   iv. If the Purchaser complies with the provisions of paragraph iii, then the Seller shall sign the release and declare this Contract void within 3
        Days or elect to provide the Specified Financing to the Purchaser, provided the lender's rejection of the loan is not for appraisal reasons.

Figure 7.1   (continued)

v. If the Seller does not elect to provide the Specified Financing, but does not sign the release and declare this Contract void when required to do so, then the Purchaser may declare the Contract void and the Deposit shall be refunded in full to the Purchaser. In the event this Contract is voided by the Seller or Purchaser under the provisions of the FINANCING CONTINGENCY paragraph, the Deposit shall be refunded in full to the Purchaser according to the terms of the DEPOSIT paragraph.

B. The Purchaser shall be in default if settlement does not occur because the Purchaser:
i.   Fails to lock-in the interest rate(s) as specified above and the rate(s) increase so that the Purchaser no longer qualifies for such financing; or
ii. Applies for, and fails to obtain, alternative financing instead of the Specified Financing, unless the Seller consents in writing to the terms of the alternative financing, in which case the alternative financing becomes the Specified Financing; or
iii. Fails to comply with the lender's requirements in a timely manner; or
iv. Fails to immediately give Notice to the Seller or the Broker of any material adverse changes in the Purchaser's assets, liabilities or income; or
v.   Does not have the down payment and closing fees to settle as provided in this Contract at the time of settlement; or
vi. Does or fails to do any act following the Contract Acceptance that prevents the Purchaser from obtaining the financing, or
vii. Makes any deliberate misrepresentations, material omissions or inaccuracies in financial information that results in the Purchaser's inability to secure the financing.

C. The Purchaser shall obtain hazard and title insurance, as required by the lender(s).

10. **PURCHASER'S REPRESENTATIONS.** The Purchaser ☐ shall, **OR** ☐ shall not occupy the Property as the Purchaser's principal residence. Unless specified in a written contingency, neither this Contract nor the financing is dependent or contingent on the sale and settlement or lease of other real property. The Selling Company ☐ is, **OR** ☐ is not authorized to disclose to the Listing Company and Seller the appropriate financial or credit information statement provided to the Selling Company by the Purchaser. The Purchaser acknowledges that the Seller is relying upon all of the Purchaser's representations including without limitation the accuracy of financial or credit information given to the Seller, Broker or the lender by the Purchaser.

11. **ACCESS TO PROPERTY.** The Seller shall provide the Broker, the Purchaser, inspectors representing the Purchaser and representatives of lending institutions for appraisal purposes, reasonable access to the Property to comply with this Contract. The Purchaser and/or the Purchaser's representative shall have the right to make a presettlement and/or a preoccupancy inspection at which time the Seller shall have all utilities in service.

12. **WELL AND SEPTIC.** If the Property is on well and/or septic systems, the ☐ Purchaser, at Purchaser's expense **OR** ☐ Seller, at Seller's expense, shall furnish the Purchaser on or before settlement with a certificate that meets the lender's requirements from the appropriate local government authority, or a private company chosen by written consent of the parties, indicating that: A. The well water contains no more than the acceptable level of contaminants and ; B. The septic system appears to be functioning satisfactorily, and if known by public records, was installed pursuant to a valid health department permit. If either system is found defective or substandard, the Seller shall take appropriate remedial action at the Seller's expense.

13. **TERMITE INSPECTION.** The Seller warrants at the time of settlement that all dwellings and/or garage(s) within the Property (excluding fences or shrubs not abutting garage(s) or dwelling(s)) are free of visible termites and other wood-destroying insects, and free from visible insect damage. The ☐ Purchaser, at Purchaser's expense **OR** ☐ Seller, at Seller's expense, shall furnish a written report to this effect acceptable to the lender from a pest control firm. Required extermination and repairs shall be at the Seller's expense.

14. **REPAIRS.** If, as a condition of providing financing under this Contract, the lender requires repairs to be made to the Property, then the Purchaser shall give Notice to the Seller of the lender's required repairs. Within 5 Days after Notice, the Seller shall give Notice to the Purchaser whether the Seller will make the repairs. If the Seller will not make the repairs, the Purchaser shall give Notice to the Seller within 5 Days after the Seller's Notice whether the Purchaser will make the repairs. If neither the Seller nor the Purchaser will make the repairs, then this Contract shall become void and the Deposit shall be refunded in full to the Purchaser. This clause will not release the Seller from any responsibilities set forth in the paragraphs entitled PERSONAL PROPERTY, FIXTURES AND UTILITIES; EQUIPMENT, MAINTENANCE AND CONDITION; WELL AND SEPTIC; TERMITE INSPECTION; or OTHER TERMS, or any terms specifically set forth in this Contract and any addenda.

15. **DAMAGE OR LOSS.** The risk of damage or loss to the Property by fire, act of God, or other casualty remains with the Seller until the execution and delivery of the deed of conveyance.

16. **TITLE.** The title report and survey, if required, shall be ordered promptly and, if not available at the scheduled date of settlement, then settlement may be delayed for up to 15 business days to obtain the title report and survey after which this Contract, at the option of the Seller, may be terminated and the Deposit shall be refunded in full to the Purchaser. Fee simple title to the Property, and everything that conveys with it, shall be sold free of liens except for any loans assumed by the Purchaser. The Seller shall comply with all orders, requirements, or notices of violations of any county or local authority, condominium unit owners' association, homeowners' or property owners' association or actions in any court on account thereof, against or affecting the Property on the date of settlement. Title is to be good and marketable, and insurable by a licensed title insurance company with no additional risk premium. Title may be subject to commonly acceptable easements, covenants, conditions and restrictions of record, if any; otherwise, the Purchaser may declare this Contract void and the Deposit shall be refunded in full, unless the defects are of such character that they may be remedied within 30 Days beyond the date of settlement set forth in the **SETTLEMENT DATE** paragraph. In case action is required to perfect the title, such action must be taken promptly by the Seller at the Seller's expense. The Broker is hereby expressly released from all liability for damages by reason of any defect in the title. The Seller shall convey the Property by general warranty deed with English covenants of title (Virginia); general warranty deed (West Virginia); special warranty deed (D.C. and Maryland). The Seller shall sign such affidavits, lien waivers, tax certifications, and other documents as may be required by the lender, title insurance company, Settlement Agent, or government authority, and authorizes the Settlement Agent to obtain pay-off or assumption information from any existing lenders.

17. **POSSESSION DATE.** Unless otherwise agreed to in writing between the Seller and the Purchaser, the Seller shall give possession of the Property at the time of settlement. If the Seller fails to do so and occupies the Property beyond the time of settlement, the Seller shall be a tenant by sufferance of the Purchaser and hereby expressly waives all notice to quit as provided by law. The Purchaser shall have the right to proceed by any legal means available to obtain possession of the Property. The Seller shall pay any damages and costs incurred by the Purchaser including reasonable attorney fees.

18. **SETTLEMENT DATE.** The Seller and the Purchaser shall make full settlement in accordance with the terms of this Contract on or, with mutual consent, before _____ , 19 ____, except as otherwise provided in this Contract.

19. **SETTLEMENT AGENT.** The Purchaser wishes to employ _____ ("Settlement Agent") to represent the Contract. Either party may retain their own counsel. The Purchaser agrees to contact the Settlement Agent within 10 Days of Contract Acceptance to schedule settlement, which Settlement Agent shall order the title exam and survey if required.

Figure 7.1   *(continued)*

20. **FEES.** Fees for the preparation of the Deed, that portion of the Settlement Agent's fee billed to the Seller, costs of releasing existing encumbrances, appropriate legal fees and any other proper charges assessed to the Seller shall be paid by the Seller. Fees for the title exam (except as otherwise provided) survey, recording (including those for any purchase money trusts) and that portion of the Settlement Agent's fee billed to the Purchaser, appropriate legal fees and any other proper charges assessed to the Purchaser shall be paid by the Purchaser. **Fees to be charged shall be reasonable and customary for the jurisdiction in which the Property is located.** (Recording, Transfer and Grantor's Taxes are covered in the appropriate jurisdictional addenda).

21. **BROKER'S FEE.** The Seller irrevocably instructs the Settlement Agent to pay the Broker compensation ("Broker's Fee") as set forth in the listing agreement and to disburse the compensation offered by the Listing Company to the Selling Company in writing as of the Contract Date, and the remaining amount of Broker's compensation to the Listing Company.

22. **ADJUSTMENTS.** Rents, taxes, water and sewer charges, front foot benefit and house connection charges, condominium unit owners' association, homeowners' and/or property owners' association regular periodic assessments (if any) and any other operating charges, are to be adjusted to the date of settlement. Any heating or cooking fuels remaining in supply tank(s) at time of settlement shall become the property of the Purchaser. Taxes, general and special, are to be adjusted according to the certificate of taxes issued by the collector of taxes, if any, except that recorded assessments for improvements completed prior to the Date of Acceptance, whether assessments have been levied or not, shall be paid by the Seller or allowance made at the time of settlement. If a Deed of Trust is assumed, interest shall be adjusted to the date of settlement and the Purchaser shall reimburse the Seller for existing escrow accounts, if any.

23. **ATTORNEY'S FEES.** In any action or proceeding involving a dispute between the Purchaser and the Seller arising out of this Contract, the prevailing party shall be entitled to receive from the other party reasonable attorney's fees to be determined by the court or arbitrator(s). In the event a dispute arises resulting in the Broker being made a party to any litigation or if the Broker is required to bring litigation to collect the Broker's Fee, the Purchaser and Seller agree to indemnify the Broker, its employees, and/or licensees for all attorney fees and costs of litigation, unless the litigation results in a judgment against the Broker, its employees and/or licensees.

24. **PERFORMANCE.** Delivery of the required funds and executed documents to the Settlement Agent shall constitute sufficient tender of performance. Funds from this transaction at settlement may be used to pay off any existing liens and encumbrances, including interest, as required by lender(s) or lienholders.

25. **DEFAULT.** If the Purchaser fails to settle as required, at the option of the Seller, the Deposit may be forfeited as liquidated damages and not as a penalty, in which event the Purchaser shall be relieved from further liability to the Seller. If the Seller does not elect to accept the Deposit as liquidated damages, the Deposit may not be the limit of the Purchaser's liability in the event of a default. If the Deposit is forfeited, or if there is an award of damages by a court or a compromise agreement between the Seller and Purchaser, the Broker may accept and the Seller agrees to pay the Broker one-half of the Deposit in lieu of the Broker's Fee, (provided Broker's share of any forfeited Deposit shall not exceed the amount due under the listing agreement). If the Seller fails to make full settlement as required, the Purchaser shall have all legal or equitable remedies, including specific performance and/or damages. If either the Seller or Purchaser refuses to execute a release of Deposit when requested to do so in writing and a court finds that they should have executed the agreement, the party who so refused to execute a release of Deposit shall pay the expenses, including, without limitation, reasonable attorney's fees, incurred by the other party in the litigation. The Seller and Purchaser agree that no Escrow Agent shall have any liability to any party on account of disbursement of the Deposit or on account of failure to disburse the Deposit, except only in the event of the Escrow Agent's gross negligence or willful misconduct. The parties further agree that the Escrow Agent shall not be liable for the failure of any depository in which the Deposit is placed and that the Seller and Purchaser each will indemnify, defend and save harmless the Escrow Agent from any loss or expense arising out of the holding, disbursement or failure to disburse the Deposit, except in the case of the Escrow Agent's gross negligence or willful misconduct. If either the Purchaser or the Seller is in default, then in addition to all other damages, the defaulting party shall immediately pay the costs incurred for the title examination, appraisal, survey and the Broker's Fee in full.

26. **OTHER DISCLOSURES. The Purchaser and Seller are advised to seek professional advice concerning the condition of the property or concerning legal and tax matters.** The following subparagraphs disclose some matters which the parties may wish to investigate further. These disclosures are not intended to create a contingency. Any contingency must be specified by adding appropriate terms to this Contract. The parties acknowledge the following disclosures:
   A. PROPERTY CONDITION. The Property is sold in "AS IS" condition except as further provided in the EQUIPMENT, MAINTENANCE AND CONDITION paragraph. Various inspection services and home warranty insurance programs are available. The Broker is not advising the parties as to certain other issues, including without limitation: water, sewer or septic; soil condition; flood hazard areas; possible restrictions of the use of the property due to restrictive covenants, zoning, subdivision, or environmental laws, easements or other documents; airport or aircraft noise; planned land use, roads or highways; and construction materials and/or hazardous materials, including without limitation flame retardant treated plywood (FRT), radon, urea formaldehyde foam insulation (UFFI), polybutylene pipes, asbestos and lead-based paint. Information relating to these issues may be available from appropriate government authorities.
   B. LEGAL REQUIREMENTS. All contracts for the sale of real property must be in writing to be enforceable. Upon Contract Acceptance, this Contract becomes a legally binding agreement. Any changes must be made by written amendment.
   C. FINANCING. Mortgage rates and associated charges vary with financial institutions and the marketplace. The Purchaser has the opportunity to select the lender and the right to negotiate terms and conditions of the financing subject to the terms of this Contract. The financing may require substantial lump sum (balloon) payments on the due dates. The Purchaser has not relied upon any representations regarding the future availability of mortgage money or interest rates for the refinancing of any such lump sum payments.
   D. BROKER. The Broker may from time to time engage in the general insurance, title insurance, mortgage loan, real estate settlement, home warranty and other real estate-related businesses and services. Therefore, in addition to the Broker's Fee specified herein, the Broker may receive compensation related to other services provided in the course of this transaction. The Purchaser and Seller acknowledge that the Broker is being retained solely as a real estate agent and is not an attorney, tax advisor, lender, appraiser, surveyor, structural engineer, home inspector or other professional service provider.

27. **ASSIGNABILITY.** This Contract may not be assigned without the written consent of the Purchaser and the Seller. If the Purchaser and Seller agree in writing to an assignment of this Contract, the original parties to this Contract remain obligated hereunder until settlement.

28. **DEFINITIONS.** "Days" means calendar days unless otherwise specified. For the purpose of computing time periods, the first Day shall be the Day following Delivery and the time period shall end at 9 p.m. on the Day specified. If a date for settlement falls on a Saturday, Sunday, or legal holiday, then the settlement shall be on the prior business day. "Contract Acceptance" means the date of final acceptance in writing of all the terms of this Contract (not the date of expiration or removal of any contingencies). "Delivery" means hand-carried, sent by overnight delivery service, by facsimile transmission, or when receipt is acknowledged in writing. In the event of overnight delivery service, Delivery shall be deemed to have been made on the Day following the sending. The masculine includes the feminine and the singular includes the plural.

Figure 7.1   *(continued)*

29. **NOTICES.** All notices ("Notice") required to be given by this Contract shall be in writing and shall be effective as of the date on which such Notice is Delivered:

    A. Addressed to the Seller at: _____ **OR**
transmitted by facsimile to (_____) _____;

    B. Addressed to the Purchaser at: _____ **OR**
transmitted by facsimile to (_____) _____.

30. **MISCELLANEOUS.** This Contract may be signed in one or more counterparts, each of which is deemed to be an original, and all of which shall together constitute one and the same instrument. Documents obtained via facsimile machines shall also be considered as originals. Typewritten or handwritten provisions included in this Contract shall control all pre-printed provisions that are in conflict. If the Contract is voided, the Deposit shall be disbursed in accordance with the DEPOSIT paragraph.

31. **ADDITIONS.** **The appropriate JURISDICTIONAL ADDENDUM must be attached and made a part of this Contract.** The following are made a part of this Contract:

☐ Yes ☐ No HOME INSPECTION ADDENDUM   ☐ Yes ☐ No LEAD - BASED PAINT DISCLOSURE FORM
☐ Yes ☐ No SALE OF HOME CONTINGENCY ADDENDUM ☐ Yes ☐ No LEAD - BASED PAINT INSPECTION CONTINGENCY
☐ Yes ☐ No RADON ADDENDUM   ☐ Yes ☐ No FHA HOME INSPECTION NOTICE
☐ Yes ☐ No HOME WARRANTY POLICY to be provided (specify): _____
☐ Yes ☐ No CONDO/COOP ADDENDUM (DC and MD)
☐ Yes ☐ No OTHER (specify): _____

_____
_____
_____

32. **OTHER TERMS.** _____

_____
_____
_____
_____
_____
_____
_____

33. **ENTIRE AGREEMENT.** This Contract shall be binding upon the parties, and each of their respective heirs, executors, administrators, successors and permitted assigns. The provisions hereof shall survive the delivery of the deed and shall not be merged therein. This Contract, unless amended in writing, contains the final and entire agreement of the parties and the parties shall not be bound by any terms, conditions, oral statements, warranties or representations not herein contained. The interpretation of this Contract shall be governed by the laws of the appropriate jurisdiction.

SELLER: **PURCHASER:**

_____/ _____ (SEAL)   _____/ _____ (SEAL)
Date   Signature   Date   Signature

_____/ _____ (SEAL)   _____/ _____ (SEAL)
Date   Signature   Date   Signature

Date and time of Contract Acceptance (see DEFINITIONS PARAGRAPH) _____, 19____ / _____ ☐ AM ☐ PM

....

For information purposes only:

Listing Company's Name and Address: Selling Company's Name and Address:

_____   _____
_____   _____
_____   _____

Associate Name _____   Associate Name _____
Office # _____ FAX # _____   Office # _____ FAX # _____
Broker Code: _____   Broker Code: _____
Sales Agent User ID # _____   Sales Agent User ID # _____

Figure 7.1 *(continued)*

CONTINGENCIES/CLAUSES ADDENDUM TO SALES CONTRACT

This Addendum is made on _____, 19 _____, to a Sales Contract ("Contract") dated _____, 19 _____ between _____("Purchaser") and _____("Seller") for the purchase and sale of the Property: _____.

The following provisions if initialed by the parties are incorporated into and made a part of this Contract:

1. CONTINGENCIES. This Contract is contingent upon the satisfaction of the contingencies set forth below ("Contingencies") until the expiration of the time periods for such Contingencies set forth below ("Deadlines"). **If each Contingency is not satisfied, removed in writing by the Deadline or terminated, then this Contract shall become void.** The parties shall sign an agreement releasing each other party from the terms of this Contract, whereupon the Deposit shall then be refunded to the Purchaser and the parties shall have no further liability under this Contract.

A. HOME INSPECTION. This Contract is contingent until **EITHER** □ 9p.m. on_____, 19_____ OR □ 9p.m., _____days after the Date of Ratification upon inspection of the Property by a professional home inspection firm at the Purchaser's expense. The Contingency will terminate at the Deadline unless the Purchaser Delivers to the Seller a written addendum listing the specific existing deficiencies together with a copy of the inspection report. The Seller may, at the Seller's option, within _____ days after Delivery of the addendum, elect in writing to remedy the deficiencies prior to settlement. If the Seller does not elect to make the repairs, or makes a counter-offer, the Purchaser shall have _____ days to respond to the counter-offer or remove this Contingency and take the Property in "as is" condition or this Contract shall become void. All of the Seller's warranties as to the condition of the Property, personal property and fixtures already in this Contract shall remain in full force and effect.

B. RADON TESTING. This Contract is contingent until **EITHER** □ 9p.m. on _____, 19_____ OR □ 9p.m., _____ days after the Date of Ratification upon the Purchaser, at the Purchaser's expense, having the property inspected for the presence of radon by a testing firm listed with the U.S. Environmental Protection Agency ("EPA") using an EPA-approved screening test method. **Testing device to be placed and retrieved by an EPA listed technician.** This Contingency will terminate at the Deadline unless the Purchaser Delivers to the Seller a written addendum stating that radon was found to be present at levels which exceed the action level established by the EPA and that this reading is not satisfactory to the Purchaser, together with a copy of the radon inspection report. The Seller may, at the Seller's option, within _____ days after receipt of the addendum, elect in writing whether or not the Seller will correct the condition. If the Seller will correct the condition, the Seller shall furnish the Purchaser with certification from the inspecting company demonstrating that the condition has been remedied before the date of settlement. If the Seller will not correct the condition, the Purchaser shall have _____ days after notice from the Seller to remove this Contingency and accept the radon condition or this Contract shall become void.

C. SALE of PURCHASER'S PROPERTY AND KICK-OUT. This Contact is contingent until **EITHER** □ 9p.m. on _____,19_____ OR □ 9 p.m., _____ days after the Date of Ratification upon the sale of the Purchaser's property located at_____ ("Purchaser's Property").

(1) The Purchaser may:
(a) satisfy this Contingency prior to the Deadline by accepting and ratifying a bona fide non-contingent (except for financing) contract for the sale of the Purchaser's Property with a settlement date specified to occur on or before the settlement date of this Contract; Delivering to the Seller or the Listing Agent a copy of such contract; and Delivery to the Seller or the Listing Agent in writing an addendum signed by the Purchaser acknowledging that this Contingency has been satisfied;
-OR-
(b) remove this Contingency prior to the Deadline by Delivering to the Seller: an addendum signed by the Purchaser removing the Contingency; evidence of funds necessary to settle on the Property; a prequalification letter from a U.S. institutional lender stating that the financing described in this Contract is available to the Purchaser and, based upon a preliminary credit report and the information provided by the Purchaser, the financing should be committed subject to appropriate verification, approval and commitment without the necessity of selling the Purchaser's Property; and copies of any other special documentation required by the lender (e.g., signed lease, signed gift letter).

(2) If the evidence listed in paragraph C(1) above is reasonably sufficient to indicate the Purchaser's financial capability to settle on the Property, then the Seller shall sign the addendum submitted by the Purchaser. If the evidence is not reasonably sufficient to indicate that the Purchaser is financially able to settle on the Property, then the Seller shall Deliver to the Purchaser a notice setting forth the reasons for the insufficiency, and this Contract shall become void. In either case, the Seller must respond in writing within _____ days after the Purchaser Delivers the documents required.

(3) Within _____ days after signing this Addendum and for the entire term of this Contingency, the Purchaser shall: (a) offer the Purchaser's Property for sale at a price not to exceed $_____; **and** (b) actively market the Purchaser's Property with a licensed real estate broker.

(4) The Seller may continue to offer the Property for sale and accept bona fide back-up offers to this Contract until this Contingency is satisfied or removed. If a back-up offer is ratified, the Seller shall Deliver notice to the Purchaser advising that this Contingency be satisfied or removed pursuant to paragraph C (1) no later than 9 p.m. on the _____ day after the date of Delivery of the notice. If this Contingency is not satisfied or removed by such time, this Contract shall become void.

(5) If it is or becomes necessary for the settlement of this Contract to coincide with the settlement of the contract for the Purchaser's Property, then the settlement under this Contract may not be delayed more than _____ days after the settlement date specified in this Contract, without the Seller's written consent. This paragraph 5 survives satisfaction of this Contingency.

Figure 7.1 *(continued)*

D. CONTINGENT ON SELLER PURCHASING ANOTHER HOME. This Contract is contingent until **EITHER** ☐ 9 p.m. on
_____, 19___ **OR** ☐ 9 p.m., _____ days after the Date of Ratification upon the Seller Delivering a notice to the Purchaser that: (1) the Seller has entered into a ratified contract to purchase another home; **OR** (2) the Seller removes this Contingency.

E. PRELIMINARY FINANCING CONTINGENCY. This Contract is contingent until **EITHER** ☐ 9p.m. on_____, 19___ **OR** ☐ 9 p.m.,_____ days after the Date of Ratification upon the Purchaser Delivering to the Seller a prequalification letter from a U.S. institutional lender stating that the financing described in this Contract is available to the Purchaser and, based upon a preliminary credit report and the information provided by the Purchaser, the financing should be committed subject to appropriate verification, approval and commitment.

F. GIFT LETTER. This Contract is contingent until **EITHER** ☐ 9 p.m. on _____, 19___ **OR** ☐ 9 p.m., _____ days after the Date of Ratification upon the Purchaser providing a gift letter satisfactory to the lender in the amount of $_____. Once the Gift Letter has been Delivered, if the Purchaser does not have the funds to settle as provided in this Contract, the Purchaser shall be in default.

G. GENERAL. This Contract is contingent until **EITHER** ☐ 9 p.m. on _____, 19___ **OR** ☐ 9 p.m., _____ days after the Date of Ratification upon _____
_____
_____
_____
_____
_____

2. **CLAUSES.**

A. BACK-UP CONTRACT OR OFFER. This Contract is first back-up to another contract or offer dated _____, 19 ____ between the Seller and _____ as purchaser and will go into full force and effect as the primary contract immediately upon notice that the first contract or offer is no longer in effect. This back-up contract is voidable by the Purchaser by Delivering notice to the Seller at any time before receipt of notice from the Seller that it has become the primary contract. If the Purchaser voids this Contract or the other contract settles, all parties shall sign the appropriate releases, the Deposit shall be refunded to the Purchaser and the parties shall have no further liability under this Contract.

B. "COINCIDING" SETTLEMENTS. Settlement of this Contract is subject to the settlement of the contract for the Purchaser's property located at _____ preceding the settlement of this Contract. Settlement under this Contract may not be delayed more than _____ days after the settlement date specified in this Contract without the parties' written consent. If a further delay is required to obtain coinciding settlements and the parties do not agree, then this Contract shall become void, all parties shall sign the appropriate releases, the Deposit shall then be refunded to the Purchaser and the parties shall have no further liability under this Contract.

C. PRE- OR POST-SETTLEMENT OCCUPANCY AGREEMENT. The parties adopt the attached occupancy agreement as part of this Contract.

Except as modified by this Addendum, all of the terms and provisions of this Contract are hereby expressly ratified and confirmed and shall remain in full force and effect.

WITNESS OUR SIGNATURES AND SEALS:
SELLER: **PURCHASER:**

_____/ _____ (SEAL)   _____/ _____ (SEAL)
Date   Signature   Date   Signature

_____/ _____ (SEAL)   _____/ _____ (SEAL)
Date   Signature   Date   Signature

Spousal Consent

If property is owned in severalty *and the owner is married,* the seller's spouse should join in the contract so that no claims can be made later. If one or both spouses do not sign, the courts will not order specific performance on the contract unless the buyer is willing to accept a deed that remains subject to the spousal interest. The buyer may still sue the seller for breach of contract since the seller could not convey the property with a clear title.

The capacity in which each signer executes the contract should be clearly stated. The contract should indicate whether the signer is an individual, a married couple, a partnership, a corporation, a limited liability company or any other legal entity.

Title

The buyer under a real estate sales contract expects to receive marketable title to the property from the seller. "Marketable title" and "insurable title" are not necessarily the same, because a title insurance policy may list exceptions against which it does not insure.

Equitable title. When the buyer and seller have executed (that is, signed) the sales contract, the buyer's interest is called *equitable title*. A buyer's equitable title gives the buyer an insurable interest in the property. While Virginia law places the risk of damage to the property during this period on the buyer, most sales contracts in Virginia provide that the seller bears the risk of loss. Licensees should ensure that this point is addressed in the contract.

WARRANTIES

As discussed in previous chapters, the principle of *caveat emptor* ("let the buyer beware") is still the law in Virginia regarding previously owned homes.

Existing Homes

In most areas, the seller will warrant that the heating, plumbing, electrical and air-conditioning systems are in working order at the time of settlement. The buyer usually has the opportunity for a walk-through inspection prior to settlement to verify that no material changes have occurred since the signing of the sales contract (such as storm damage, vandalism or the removal of fixtures). If there have been any changes, the seller is required to inform the buyer of them, regardless of whether a walk-through is to be performed. It is a buyer's responsibility to determine what conditions beyond the property's boundaries may affect its value.

New Construction

For new homes, the builder normally supplies a detailed warranty, primarily to limit his or her liability, which includes a five-year warranty against foundation defects. At the time of closing, there is an implied warranty that the dwelling and its fixtures (to the seller's best actual knowledge) are free from structural defects and constructed in a professional manner. A *structural defect* is a flaw that reduces the stability or safety of the structure below accepted standards or that restricts the normal use of the structure. The implied warranties continue for one year after the date of transfer of title or the buyer's taking possession, whichever occurs first.

Questions

1. The buyer and seller agree to the sale of Blackacre for $100,000. No written contract is signed, but the seller accepts payment in full from the buyer and delivers the deed. Which of the following statements is true?

    a. The sale is without legal effect; the seller continues to own Blackacre.
    b. The sale violates the Statute of Frauds' maximum amount for oral contracts.
    c. The sale is enforceable in a court of law under the Statute of Frauds, due to the parties' compliance.
    d. The sale is unenforceable under the Statute of Frauds, but the parties are free to comply with its terms.

2. Two weeks after a buyer and seller signed a sales contract on a house, the house burned to the ground. If the contract is silent on the issue, which party is liable?

    a. The buyer only, under his or her equitable title interest.
    b. The buyer and seller share the risk of loss equally.
    c. The seller, because he or she continues to possess title to the property.
    d. The seller, under the implied condition of good faith.

3. D built a house with the intention of selling it. During construction, the foundation cracked and D was forced to build the bearing walls of a lighter material to keep the entire structure from collapsing. D's engineer told D that a strong wind would probably blow the house down. Nonetheless, the cracked foundation and structural shortcuts were easily covered over, and D sold the house to a first-time homebuyer without mentioning the defects. Two weeks after closing, the house collapsed in a thunderstorm. Is D liable?

    a. No, under *caveat emptor*.
    b. No, because the buyer never asked about specific defects.
    c. Yes; due to the implied warranty against structural defects.
    d. Yes, due to the failure to have the property inspected.

4. P owns a vacation cabin in the Blue Ridge Mountains. K stops by P's house and asks to rent the cabin from February through December for $550 per month. P agrees. If K fails to make the rent payments, is the contract enforceable?

    a. No; an oral contract for the sale or lease of real estate is enforceable.
    b. No; contracts for more than $5,000 must be in writing to be enforceable.
    c. Yes; the Statute of Frauds applies only to the sale of real property.
    d. Yes; an oral lease for a term of less than one year is enforceable.

8 Transfer of Title

REQUIREMENTS FOR A VALID CONVEYANCE

In Virginia, the requirements for a valid deed are:

- Grantor who has the legal capacity to execute the deed
- Grantee
- Consideration
- Granting clause
- Accurate legal description of the property
- Any relevant exceptions or reservations
- Signature of the grantor, sometimes with acknowledgment
- Delivery and acceptance of the deed

Grantor

In Virginia, the same person may be the grantor and grantee in a deed.

Grantee

The grantee named to receive a deed to real property should be legally competent to receive the property. The grantee's full name should be used in preparing the deed. A deed to a nonexistent person is a valid conveyance to the intended but misnamed grantee if the intended grantee exists and the intention of the parties can be determined.

Competence

The grantor is presumed to have been competent at the time a deed was executed. The test of legal capacity is the party's mental ability to understand the nature and consequences of the transaction at the time it is entered into. The burden of proving incompetence is on the party who attacks the validity of the deed.

In Virginia, a conveyance of land by a minor is a valid transfer of title, unless it is repudiated by the minor after he or she attains majority. Repudiation may occur even though the grantee has already conveyed the property to another purchaser without notice that a minor was the grantor in the previous transaction.

Habendum Clause

The *habendum clause*, "to have and to hold," is rarely used in Virginia.

Power of Attorney

If a seller or buyer is unable to attend the closing, there are two options:

1. Prepare all papers to be signed in advance of the closing or

2. Use a *power of attorney*

A power of attorney must be signed by the seller with the same formalities as a deed. Although a power of attorney can be general or specific, *a specific power of attorney is required to convey real property in Virginia.* In reviewing a power of attorney, the licensee should have a lawyer verify that it specifically authorizes performance of all necessary acts, and that the attorney-in-fact performs in accordance with the authority granted in the power of attorney.

Affidavits and other sworn statements cannot be signed by the attorney-in-fact. These must be signed by the principal prior to the closing. The deed or other instrument to be signed must indicate that it is being signed by an attorney-in-fact. Normally this is accomplished by a recital in the body of the instrument or under the signature line.

If an institutional lender is making a new loan, the lender's permission should be obtained for a borrower to execute a power of attorney. The lender may not allow the use of an attorney-in-fact, especially if the loan is subject to truth-in-lending requirements.

A power of attorney must be recorded, and the recording fees are charged to the party using the attorney-in-fact. If the power of attorney is not recorded, it is as though the deed were unsigned by the party being represented by the attorney-in-fact.

TRANSFER TAXES AND FEES

Recordation Tax

With certain exceptions, all deeds are subject to state and city or county recording tax. The state tax is currently $.15 per $100 (or fraction of $100) of the consideration paid or the value of the property, whichever is greater. The county or city tax is one-third of that amount, or $.05 per $100 (or fraction of $100).

These taxes are usually paid by the buyer and collected at closing. Payment of these taxes is a prerequisite to having the deed recorded.

Grantor Tax

In addition to the recordation taxes, all deeds are subject to a grantor's tax of $.50 per $500 (or a fraction of $500) of the purchase price or the value of the grantor's equity in the property being transferred, in the case of assumption. The grantor's tax is paid by the seller and is collected at closing and paid to the clerk of the county where the deed is recorded.

MATH CONCEPT . . .
Calculating Virginia Transfer Taxes

Bob purchases Sue's home for $175,600

I. STATE AND CITY RECORDATION TAX

$175,600 ÷ 100 = 1,756 "recordation tax units"

Bob will pay $263.40 in state recordation taxes (1,756 x $.15 = $263.40) and $87.80 in county or city recordation tax (1,756 x $.05 = $87.80)

II. GRANTOR TAX

$175,600 ÷ 500 = 351.2

351.2 = 351 *500's*, + 1 fraction of 500 = 352 "grantor tax units"

Sue's grantor tax is 352 x $.50 = $176

Tax on Deeds of Trust and Mortgages

Unless exempted, deeds of trust and mortgages are taxed on a sliding scale, according to the amount of the obligation (that is, the debt) that the instrument secures. If the amount is not ascertainable, the tax is based on the fair market value of the property, including the value of any improvements as of the date of the deed. Deeds of trust are also subject to city or county recordation taxes, clerk's fees and any plat recordation fees.

Deeds of trust that secure both construction loans and permanent loans are normally subject to tax on deeds of trust.

Transfer Fee

For each document admitted to record, the clerk of court collects a transfer fee that is generally paid by the buyer.

Clerk Fee

In addition to the transfer fee, the clerk of court collects a fee for recording plats, powers of attorney, certificates of satisfaction and release of judgments. The amount of the fee is usually based on the number of pages that must be recorded.

The buyer generally pays the fees to record the "new" items, and the seller pays for the release of the "old" items. The payment of fees is usually negotiable.

ADVERSE POSSESSION

To establish title to land by adverse possession in Virginia, it is necessary to show actual, hostile, exclusive, visible and continuous possession of property for the statutory period of *15 years*. The possession by the defendant must be actual and continuous: more than just a sporadic taking of timber or occasional camping is required. The adverse possession must be exclusive to constitute an ouster of the true owner.

When several persons enter upon land in succession, these possessions cannot be "tacked" to preserve the essential continuity unless there is a "privity of estate" between them. In other words, the intent to establish a continuous succession of adverse possessors must be proven.

Adverse possession cannot be claimed if the possession has been abandoned by the claimant during the required time period. The occupancy necessary to support a claim of title of adverse possession must be hostile and without the true owner's permission.

TRANSFER OF A DECEASED PERSON'S PROPERTY

When any person with title to real estate that may be inherited dies testate (that is, having executed a legal will), the real estate will pass according to the terms of the instrument.

In Virginia, circuit courts serve as probate courts. Normally there is a probate section in the clerk's office where wills, lists of heirs, affidavits and other documents related to probate are located. As with other documents, a "will index" is located in the circuit courts.

IN PRACTICE . . .
When a licensee lists a property that is part of a decedent's estate, he or she should establish that the rate of commission to be paid has been approved by the court handling the probate.

Until probate, the will is only the legal declaration of a person's intended disposition. A will may be revoked at any time after execution, while a deed cannot be revoked after it has been delivered to the grantee. The rule of construction in determining whether an instrument is a will or a contract is that if it passes a *present interest*, it is a deed or contract; but if its rights or interests do not convey until the death of the maker, it is a testamentary paper, or will.

Validity

A testator can only have one last will and testament. A will may be set aside for fraud, undue influence, force or coercion.

No person of unsound mind or under the age of 18 years is capable of making a valid will. Virginia law only requires testamentary capacity at the time the will is made; the testator's subsequent capacity is not relevant.

Neither the testator's poor health or impaired intellect is sufficient, standing alone, to render a will invalid.

No will is valid unless it is in writing. A valid will must be signed by the testator or by some other person in the testator's presence and by his or her direction in such a way as to make it clear that the name is intended as his or her signature. A will is also valid that is wholly in the testator's handwriting (a *holographic will*) if the testator signs the will and acknowledges it in the presence of at least two competent witnesses who are both present at the same time. These witnesses also must sign the will in the presence of the testator. The testamentary intent must appear on the face of the paper itself. Virginia law is silent on the subject of oral (unwritten) or deathbed (nuncupative) wills.

IN PRACTICE . . .

When representing the purchaser of property from a decedent's estate, or in taking a listing of estate property, it is wise to request a certified copy of the will and determine whether the executor under the will has the power of sale. Where the executor does *not* have the power of sale, or in dealing with an intestate's property, all the heirs and their spouses must execute a deed as grantors conveying the property to the grantee.

Questions

1. An heir was to have inherited real property under his uncle's will. However, the uncle sold the property shortly before he died. The heir now wants to have the sale rescinded on grounds of the uncle's incompetence. Will the heir win?

   a. Yes; any such pleading by a close relative will prevail in court.
   b. Yes; the grantor would have had to prove competence in court during his or her lifetime.
   c. No; a deed can be invalidated due to incompetence only during the grantor's lifetime.
   d. No; a person is presumed competent unless a court has ruled otherwise.

2. *K*, a minor, inherited the Blackacre estate and immediately sold it to *W*, who believed that *K* was 23 years old. *W* then sold the property to *X*. Two years later, *K* repudiated the sale of Blackacre. Which of the following is true?

   a. *K*'s repudiation is without effect, because *W* no longer owns the property.
   b. *K*'s original sale of Blackacre was voidable by *K*, and *K* may recover the property from *X*.
   c. Because *W* believed that *K* was not a minor, the sale cannot be invalidated.
   d. A minor cannot repudiate the sale of real property in Virginia.

3. Which of the following would most likely invalidate a deed?

   a. Grantee's name misspelled
   b. Property description consisting of street address, city and state
   c. Failure of all grantors to sign
   d. Failure of all grantees to sign

4. If the grantor in a deed intends to retain a life estate in the property, what would be the title of the part of the contract where this condition would be found?

   a. Legal Description
   b. Habendum Clause
   c. Consideration
   d. Exceptions

5. The seller in a transaction was called out of town on business the day before the closing. Any affidavits or sworn statements the seller is required to deliver at the closing may be signed by

   a. the seller.
   b. the seller's attorney-in-fact.
   c. the buyer's attorney.
   d. the seller's real estate agent.

6. A property sold for $192,745. Which of the following is a correct statement of the taxes to be paid?

   a. Seller will pay $385.60; Buyer will pay $192.74
   b. Buyer will pay $385.60; Seller will pay $193
   c. Buyer will pay $385.55; Seller will pay $192.75
   d. Seller will pay $386; Buyer will pay $193

7. All of the following are entitled to prevail on a claim of title by adverse possession, *EXCEPT:*

   a. A person who has been in possession of the property for 19 years.
   b. A person who held the property for five years after "inheriting" it from a parent, who was in adverse possession for ten years.
   c. A person who has been entering an orchard and taking apples every October since 1972.
   d. A person who has been parking his or her car on a neighbor's property for 20 years without permission.

8. *K* was very ill, and so wrote a will in her own handwriting, leaving all her property to *L*. Three witnesses heard *K* say, "This is my will." The witnesses watched *K*'s friend sign *K*'s name to the document, because *K* was too exhausted to do it herself. "That's as good as my signature," *K* said weakly. The witnesses signed the will. What is the status of this document?

   a. The will is invalid because Virginia does not recognize holographic wills.
   b. The will is valid.
   c. The will is invalid, because *K* did not sign it herself.
   d. The will is valid, but cannot be enforced because it is a nuncupative will.

9 Title Records

TITLE EXAMINATIONS

The real estate licensee should furnish the purchaser's attorney with a copy of the contract of sale, information concerning any unrealized deeds of trust (whether they are to be satisfied prior to closing or not), any existing title insurance policies (or "back title letters") and any known unrecorded deeds or other liens or encumbrances on the property. The seller is not required to have marketable title until the time of closing and must be given a reasonable time to correct any defects found before settlement. In any letter to the seller, the buyer's attorney should merely point out any known title problems. If the settlement date is important, the letter should specify a date and may state that "time is of the essence."

Wet Settlement Act

The Virginia Wet Settlement Act requires that the deed of trust and any other documents be recorded, and all settlement proceeds be distributed, within two business days of the date of settlement. [§6.1-2.13] The Wet Settlement Act applies only to transactions involving loans made by lenders that will be secured by first deeds of trust or mortgages on real estate containing four or fewer residential dwelling units.

Procedure

In a title examination, the prospective seller's chain of title is developed by searching through the grantee index backward in time to some predetermined point to establish the source of title for each owner in the chain. Then, for each grantor in the chain of title, the examiner searches the grantor's index from the date the grantor acquired title to the date it was transferred to the next grantor in the chain. This process, called *adversing the title,* is done to determine whether any person not in the seller's direct chain of title might have some adverse claim or interest recorded against the property to be conveyed.

Finally, the examiner will search other indexes to determine whether there are any unrecorded claims against the property, such as judgment liens, mechanics' liens or tax liens. While real estate licensees do not perform a title search in the normal course of taking a listing, they should alert the parties' attorneys in the event of even the slightest hint of title issues.

Title examinations may be classified as full or limited searches. In a *full search*, the seller's title must be established for at least 60 years. A *limited search* is a title examination that goes back fewer than 60 years. Limited searches are appropriate for some loan assumptions and second mortgage closings, unless the second mortgagee requires lender's title insurance.

A chain of title consists of consecutive terms of ownership: a gap in the chain could be caused by an unrecorded deed, a name change, an unadministered estate, a foreign divorce decree or some other circumstance. Unless the missing link can be reconstructed from reliable sources, the defect could destroy the closing.

Errors such as an erroneous legal description, a misspelled name or an improper execution in a prior recorded deed in the seller's chain of title must be corrected before the closing can proceed. Where possible, these problems can be cured by a correction deed from the same grantor to the same grantee; the correction deed must be recorded. A correction deed may not be used to change a greater estate to a lesser estate, nor can it be used to change the identity of the grantor altogether. It is the responsibility of the seller to locate the parties, then to correct the deed.

Title Report

At a minimum, the title report should reveal:

- title holder of record;
- legal description of property;
- existing lenders;
- other lienholders (such as mechanics' lienors, judgment lienors and tax liens);
- status of taxes;
- easements, covenants and other restrictions;
- objections to marketability;
- other matters affecting title; and
- requirements for vesting marketable title in the purchaser.

TITLE INSURANCE

Settlement agents are required by Virginia law to advise purchasers and borrowers of the availability of owner title insurance, and of the benefits of acquiring it. It is to the benefit of the purchaser to have title insurance because the premium paid is nominal compared with the potential cost an owner could incur in connection with a suit to quiet title or other litigation regarding a defect in title.

TITLE ISSUES

Judgment Liens

Judgments constitute liens against all real property that the defendant owns or subsequently acquires. If the seller denies being named in the judgment, and it is not certain that the judgment is against the seller, an affidavit to this effect may be sufficient to protect the purchaser.

Judgments against prior owners of property may remain as valid liens against the property despite the fact that the property has been subsequently conveyed. The purchaser should require the seller to satisfy all judgments against the property, because they remain as liens against the property for 20 years and are subject to execution.

Deed of Trust

A real estate licensee should be aware that it is not unusual for a title examiner to discover an unreleased deed of trust on the property. Most often, this is due to the failure of the lender or closer to have a certificate of satisfaction or deed of release signed by the beneficiary and recorded in a timely manner. Unreleased deeds of trust often go unnoticed until the seller attempts to sell the property. When the lender was a bank or mortgage company and the lien was in fact paid off, it is relatively easy to have a certificate of satisfaction executed and recorded prior to closing. However, if an individual or private lender was involved, these situations can cause delays in the closing, primarily owing to the problems associated with locating the individual.

Mechanics' Liens

Reported mechanics' or materialmen's liens must be treated as adverse claims against the property. The purchaser should require that these liens be paid and satisfied of record or discharged by the filing of a proper bond at or prior to closing. Unreported liens are also of concern to the purchaser, who will take the property subject to all mechanics' and materialmen's liens for work or materials furnished within the last 90 days. For this reason the purchaser should require that the seller provide an affidavit that there have been no improvements performed or materials supplied within the 90 days prior to the date of closing. This affidavit, commonly known as a "90-day letter," is required by all lenders and title insurance companies.

Mechanics' liens are generally not covered by standard title insurance. However, insurance carriers will provide this coverage for an additional premium.

Questions

1. When is the seller of real property required to have marketable title?

   a. At the time the listing is taken
   b. When a sales contract is signed
   c. By the time the buyer's loan is approved
   d. At closing

2. *B* is purchasing property from *S*. Prior to closing, certain defects are found in *S*'s title. What is the status of the sales contract between these parties?

   a. It is automatically rescinded.
   b. The seller has a reasonable time to correct defects, so the contract is still in effect.
   c. The buyer may, at his or her option, cancel the contract and recover the earnest money.
   d. The contract is in force, and the buyer must close the transaction and accept the transfer as long as the defects are curable.

3. What is the primary requirement of Virginia's Wet Settlement Act?

   a. Documents must be recorded and disbursements made within two business days of settlement.
   b. Documents can be recorded only if funds were disbursed at settlement.
   c. Recording of documents can occur only with actual notice of disbursement of funds.
   d. Recording of deeds is not necessary if the deed is a deed of gift.

4. All of the following are reasons why a listing agent should ask to see all documents the seller has concerning the property at the time of taking the listing, *EXCEPT*:

   a. to find out about unrecorded deeds.
   b. to verify deed of trust loan numbers and payment status.
   c. to learn of any liens that may not be recorded.
   d. to fulfill the requirement that a seller have marketable title at the time a property is held out for sale.

5. A full title search goes back how many years?

   a. 20   c. 60
   b. 40   d. 80

6. All of the following are protections offered to an insured by a standard title insurance policy, *EXCEPT*

   a. Losses suffered because of defects in the record title
   b. Hidden defects not disclosed by the public record
   c. The cost of defending the title against adverse claims
   d. Mechanics' and materialmens' liens.

7. Which of the following changes may not be accomplished by using a correction deed?

    a. A change from a fee simple to a life estate
    b. Correction of an erroneous legal description
    c. Respelling of a misspelled name
    d. Correcting the signature on an improperly executed deed

8. In cases where title must be cleared by having correction deeds signed, who is responsible for locating the parties who must sign?

    a. The buyer
    b. The seller
    c. The closing lawyer
    d. The real estate licensee who represents the owner.

VIRGINIA REAL ESTATE LICENSE LAW

Virginia Code §54.1, Chapter 21, is the section of the statute that governs the practice of real estate professionals. The purpose of the law is to protect the public interest against fraud, misrepresentation, dishonesty and incompetence in real estate transactions.

The law designates the Real Estate Board (REB) as the authority with the power to enforce, amend and promulgate rules and regulations for implementing the law.

Definitions [LL§54.1-2100 et seq.; 18 VAC 135-20-10]

Certain words and phrases are used throughout both the License Law and the Rules and Regulations of the Real Estate Board (REB). These words and phrases have specific, statutory meanings separate and apart from any definition they might have outside the real estate profession.

Actively Engaged — Employment by, or affiliation as, an independent contractor with a licensed real estate firm or sole proprietor in performing acts of real estate brokerage for an average of 40 hours per week.

Associate Broker — An individual, licensed by the REB as a broker, other than one who has been designated as the principal broker. An associate broker is required to meet the same educational, experience and testing requirement as a principal broker. An associate broker, because of his or her affiliation with a firm or sole proprietorship, is subject to the same restriction of brokerage activity as a salesperson.

Client — An individual who has entered into a brokerage relationship with a licensee.

Firm — Any sole proprietorship (nonbroker owner) partnership, association, limited liability company, or corporation, other than a sole proprietorship (principal broker owned), that is required by regulation to obtain a separate brokerage firm license.

Inactive Status — Any broker or salesperson who is not under the supervision of a principal broker or supervising broker, who is not affiliated with a firm or sole proprietorship, who is not performing any real estate activities, and whose license is held with the REB.

Independent Contractor — A licensee who acts for or represents a client other than as a standard agent and whose duties and obligations are governed by a written contract between licensee and the client.

Licensee — Any person, partnership, association, corporation or limited liability company that holds a real estate license.

Principal Broker — The individual broker designated by each firm to ensure compliance with the Virginia Real Estate License Law and related rules and regulations, as well as to receive communications and notices from the REB that may affect the firm or any licensee employed or affiliated with the firm. The principal broker has responsibility for the activities of the firm and all its licensees. In the case of a sole proprietorship, the licensed broker who is the sole proprietor has the responsibilities of the principal broker.

Principal to a Transaction — Any party to a real estate transaction in the capacity of a seller, buyer, lessee or lessor.

Real Estate — As defined in the Virginia law, real estate includes condominiums, leaseholds, time-sharing and any other interest in real property. Ownership of a cooperative apartment is also considered real estate ownership, even though the shares held by members of the co-op are construed as personal property.

Sole Proprietor — Any individual, not a corporation, who is trading under his or her own name or under a fictitious or assumed name, as provided by the regulations.

Standard Agent — A licensee who acts for or represents a client in an agency relationship and who is obligated to adhere to the Virginia Real Estate License Law.

Supervising Broker — The individual broker designated by the firm to supervise the activities of any one of the firm's offices.

THE REAL ESTATE BOARD (REB) [LL§54.1-2104, 2105]

The REB is composed of nine members. Seven members may be either brokers or salespersons with at least five consecutive years' experience immediately prior to appointment, and two are citizen (consumer) members. Appointments are made by the Governor for a term of four years. Sitting members may be reappointed for one additional four-year term. Members of the REB select the chairperson.

Authority

The REB, by statute, may do all things necessary and convenient for carrying into effect the provisions of the law. REB's authority includes

- issuing and renewing real estate licenses;

- enforcing the license law;

- taking disciplinary action for violations of license law or rules and regulations by
  - suspending or revoking a license,
  - levying fines, or
  - denying license renewal;

- establishing requirements for real estate licensing;

- approving schools for teaching authorized courses for real estate brokers and salespersons;

- determining license fees; and

- waiving all or part of the prelicense requirements if an applicant for licensure is currently licensed in another state or the District of Columbia.

In addition to administering the real estate license law, the REB has the responsibility of administering

- the Virginia Fair Housing Act;

- the Virginia Condominium Act;

- the Virginia Time-Share Act;

- the Virginia Real Estate Transaction Recovery Fund; and

- the Virginia Cooperative Act.

There are some aspects of real estate practice with which the REB does *not* become involved. For example, REB

- does not arbitrate disputes between salespersons and brokers.

- does not become involved in disputes between brokers.

- does not establish commission rates or commission splits.

- does not standardize listing agreements, sales contacts or any other forms used in the industry.

The REB could become involved in any of these matters in case of a violation of the license law or the rules and regulations.

WHO MUST HAVE A LICENSE?
[LL§54.1-2106.1; 18 VAC 135-20-20]

Any person, firm, partnership, association, limited liability company (LLC) or corporation who, for a fee, commission or other valuable consideration, performs an act of real estate brokerage for others, is required by Virginia law to be a licensed real estate broker or salesperson. The phrase, "act of real estate brokerage" includes: selling or offering real estate for sale; buying or offering to buy real estate; negotiating the purchase or exchange of real estate; and renting, leasing or negotiating a lease for real estate. Licensees may incorporate or form an LLC; however, no partnership, association, LLC or corporation may be granted a license unless every member or officer (or manager of an LLC) who actively participates in brokerage activities holds a broker's license. A

single performance of any one of these acts requires a real estate license.

Operating Without a License

If the REB is aware of someone who is engaging in acts of real estate brokerage without a license, it will investigate the matter. If the suspicion is true, the REB will refer the matter to the Commonwealth Attorney for action. Any penalty for such activities against the individual or firm will be determined by the court. Operating without a license is considered to be a Class I misdemeanor. A third or subsequent violation within a single three-year period constitutes a Class 6 felony.

REQUIREMENTS FOR LICENSURE
[18 VAC 135-20-30 through 135-20-60]

The following general requirements apply for any person seeking licensure either as a salesperson or broker, or for licensure by reciprocity. The applicant must

- be at least 18 years old;

- if licensed in another jurisdiction, be in good standing in every jurisdiction where licensed;

- have a good reputation for honesty, truthfulness and fair dealing, and be competent to transact real estate business in such a manner as to safeguard the public interest;

- not have been found guilty of violating the fair housing laws of Virginia or any other jurisdiction;

- meet the current educational requirements by achieving a passing grade in all required courses before sitting for the licensing exam and applying for licensure;

- pass a written license examination approved by the REB within 12 months prior to applying for a license and follow all rules established by the REB or the testing service regarding the conduct of license applicants, including any written or verbal instructions communicated prior to the examination date or at the test site;

- be in good standing, and not have had a real estate license suspended, revoked or surrendered in connection with a disciplinary action, or been the subject of disciplinary action in any jurisdiction;

- not have been convicted, in any jurisdiction, for a misdemeanor involving moral turpitude, sexual offense, drug distribution, physical injury or any felony. (A plea of *nolo contendere* ("no contest") is considered a conviction.)

- follow all rules established by the REB with regard to conduct at the examination.

An applicant for a broker's license must meet additional educational requirements and must have been actively engaged as a real estate salesperson for 36 of the previous 48 months.

The specific licensing requirements for a broker, salesperson and reciprocal licenses are discussed later in this chapter.

If a license applicant has had a real estate license suspended, revoked or surrendered in connection with a disciplinary action or has been subject to disciplinary action in any jurisdiction, the applicant must include a detailed explanation of the circumstances that caused the action, along with his or her application for licensure.

If an applicant has been convicted of a misdemeanor involving moral turpitude, sexual offense, drug distribution or physical injury, or any other felony, the following must be submitted with the license application:

- An official FBI record, the original state police criminal record and certified copies of court papers relative to the conviction.

- A written account of the part that he or she played in the offense, and the current status or resolution of the final conviction. If a prospective licensee is concerned about becoming licensed due to a past criminal conviction, the applicant must first meet the educational and testing requirements for licensure. The documentation is submitted with the license application.

Real Estate Examination

All initial applications for licensure must be made within 12 months of the examination date. Failure to apply within this time period will require retaking the exam.

Real Estate Salesperson

An applicant for licensure as a real estate salesperson must, in addition to the general requirements discussed above, have successfully completed a "Principles of Real Estate" or similar course approved by the REB. The course must contain 4 semester credit hours or a minimum of 60 classroom, correspondence, or other distance learning instruction hours prior to making application for the examination.

Real Estate Broker

Applicants for a real estate broker's license must meet requirements in addition to meeting the salesperson licensing requirements. An applicant must

- have been actively engaged as a real estate salesperson for 36 of the 48 months immediately preceding the date of application for licensure as a real estate broker, and

- have successfully completed 12 classroom or correspondence semester credit hours (four 45-hour courses, or 180 classroom hours) of study approved by the REB in such subjects as brokerage, real estate law, real estate investments, real estate finance, and real estate appraisal or related approved subjects prior to the licensing examination.

Applicants may ask the REB to determine the acceptability of related courses.

Concurrent Licenses

Brokers who are active in more than one legal entity (that is, who work for more than one brokerage firm) may apply for concurrent licenses. Concurrent licenses will be issued to brokers who provide written affidavits stating that written notice of the applicant's concurrent status has been provided to the principal broker of each firm with which the applicant is or will be associated.

Concurrent licensure does not refer to persons holding licenses in multiple states.

Branch Office Licenses

A successful real estate broker often has offices in several different markets. When a broker maintains multiple offices within Virginia, a *branch office license* must be issued for each branch office. The application form must include the name of the firm, the location of the branch office, and the name of the branch office's supervising broker.

Active and Inactive Licenses

An *active license* means that the licensee is affiliated with a broker. The licensee's broker must certify his or her license application, and agrees to be responsible for the licensee's brokerage activities. When the REB has approved the application, the license will be issued and sent to the broker. The licensee is now considered to have *active* status: he or she is licensed to engage in real estate activities, and receives a "pocket card" as evidence of his or her status as a broker or salesperson.

Alternatively, an individual may satisfy all the licensing requirements and pass the license examination, but choose to apply for *inactive* license status. Although the person has a license, he or she does not affiliate with a broker, and *may not* engage in acts of brokerage or earn compensation, including referral fees.

Active to Inactive Status. Any licensee may request that his or her license be placed on inactive status, which means that the licensee is no longer affiliated with any broker.

If a licensee changes from active to inactive status, it is the responsibility of the individual licensee to make application for the change and to request that the broker return the actual license. The REB, on receipt of the change of status application, notifies the former broker of the change request. If the broker has not yet returned the license of the individual involved in the change, the broker must do so within ten days.

No licensees shall engage in acts of real estate brokerage or earn compensation while their licenses are on inactive status.

Inactive to Active Status. When a licensee whose license is on inactive status affiliates with a broker, proper application must be made to have the license activated. This is accomplished by filling out an application form, having the broker certify the application and mailing the form with the proper fees to the REB. If a licensee has been on inactive status for three years or more, the licensee must meet educational requirements in effect at that time to be reinstated to active status. If the licensee was engaged in a real estate related field while he or she was inactive and can demonstrate to the REB that the knowledge of real estate has been retained, the REB may waive the education requirements. If the licensee was on inactive status at the time the license was renewed, the licensee must submit evidence that he or she did complete successfully the required continuing education course during the 24 months preceding reactivation.

Referral Agents

A referral agent is a real estate licensee who does not engage in real estate activities such as listing and selling property. As the title implies, a referral agent refers prospective buyers or sellers to the broker with whom the agent is affiliated. If a sale results from the referral, the broker may pay the licensee a fee for the referral. The referral agent's license is displayed in the referral office of the broker with whom he or she is affiliated. The REB considers a person acting in the capacity of a referral agent to be active, not inactive.

LICENSURE BY RECIPROCITY [18 VAC 135-20-60]

A person who holds a real estate license issued by another state may apply to the REB for a license by reciprocity. Applicants may obtain a Virginia real estate license by reciprocity if they:

- are at least 18 years old;

- have received the salesperson or broker's license by passing a licensing examination that is substantially equivalent to Virginia's examination;

- within 12 months prior to applying for a Virginia real estate license, have passed a written examination covering Virginia real estate license law and the regulations of the REB and have followed all rules regarding conduct at the examination;

- are in good standing as a licensed broker or salesperson in their state and have not have been subject to suspension, revocation or surrender of their license in connection with a disciplinary proceeding;

- have been actively engaged in real estate practice for 12 of the preceding

36 months, or have met educational requirements substantially equivalent to Virginia's; and

- satisfy the reputation and criminal record requirements demanded of licensees in Virginia.

Note that broker applicants must meet both education and experience requirements to be granted a license by reciprocity. However, salesperson candidates need only meet the educational requirements.

Consent to Suits

One additional requirement for nonresidents is that they file an irrevocable *consent to suits and services.* A consent to suits is a binding legal agreement to allow the Director of Professional and Occupational Regulation to accept service of any legal process or pleading on the nonresident licensee's behalf.

The service of legal documents on the director is as valid and binding on the licensee as if service had been made on the licensee in person. [§54.1-2111]

LICENSURE OF BUSINESS ENTITIES [18 VAC 135-20-45]

A partnership, association, limited liability company or corporation engaged in real estate brokerage must obtain a real estate license prior to transacting real estate business. The license application must disclose the name under which the licensee intends to do business and by which it will be known to the public. The entity's license is issued in that name. This license is separate and distinct from any license issued to any member of the firm.

Every individual member, partner, trustee, manager or officer of the organization who is engaged in the brokerage business must be licensed as a broker. Every employee who renders professional services in the name of the firm must have a real estate license. Every office, including branch offices, must be managed by the broker or an associate broker.

Partnerships and Associations

A partnership or association acting as a real estate broker must file a certificate that discloses the following information:

- the name, business address and home address of each person in the partnership or association;

- the name and style of the partnership or association;

- the address of the partnership's or association's Virginia office; and

- the length of time for which it is to continue.

Any change in the partnership or association must be filed with the REB within 30 days of the effective date of the change.

Corporations

Any corporation acting as a real estate broker must be authorized to do business in Virginia. The corporation must file a certificate with the REB that discloses

- the name, business and home addresses of each officer;

- the corporation's name and style;

- the corporation's Virginia address and its place of business.

Every change in officers must be disclosed to the REB within 30 days of the effective date of the change.

Limited Liability Companies (LLCs)

Any limited liability company (LLC) acting as a real estate broker must be authorized to do business in Virginia. The LLC must file a certificate with the REB that discloses:

- the name, business address and home address of each manager;

- the name and style of the LLC; and

- the LLC's Virginia address.

Every change in officers must be disclosed to the REB within 30 days of the effective date of the change.

RENEWAL OF LICENSES [18 VAC 135-20-90 through 135-20-130]

The real estate licenses of salespersons, brokers and firms expire every two years, on the last day of the month in which the license was issued. For a licensee to continue his or her professional real estate activities, the license must be renewed. Renewal requirements apply to active and inactive licensees alike.

The REB reserves the right to deny the renewal or reinstatement of any license for the same reasons that it would deny initial licensure or discipline a current licensee.

The Renewal Process

The REB mails renewal notices (usually 45 to 60 days prior to expiration) to each licensee at the last known home address of that individual. Renewal notices for firms are mailed to the last known business address. *Failure to receive a notice of renewal does not relieve the licensee of the responsibility to renew.*

The applicant for renewal completes the application form and returns it to the REB, along with the required fee and any other documentation that may be required. The application form and fees must be *received* by the REB prior to the expiration date that appears on the license.

If the licensee does not renew his or her license prior to expiration it is necessary to apply to have the license reinstated.

The regulations allow for reinstatement of a license up to one (1) year following expiration. If the application to reinstate is received within 30 days of expiration, there is no monetary penalty. However, from the 31st day up to 1 year, application for reinstatement is subject to a $100 fee. The $100 reinstatement fee is a flat fee and is *not* in addition to the normal renewal fees.

After 12 months, reinstatement is not possible under any circumstances, and the licensee must meet all educational and examination requirements in effect at that time and apply for licensure as a new applicant.

Once the license has expired the licensee may *not* engage in any acts of real estate brokerage or receive compensation until the license has been reinstated. Licensees who engage in acts of real estate brokerage after their licenses have expired are legally subject to the penalties associated with operating without a license. This applies even during the reinstatement period. On the date a license expires, the licensee is out of business until the license is reinstated.

Continuing Education
[18 VAC 135-20-100]

As a condition of renewing their licenses, all active real estate brokers and salespersons, whether or not they are Virginia residents, must complete one or more continuing education courses, totaling at least eight hours, during each licensing term. Licensees who are called to active duty in the United States armed forces must complete the continuing education requirement within six months of their release.

The course or courses must be provided by an accredited university, college, community college or other accredited institution of higher learning, or an approved proprietary school (that is, a privately-owned school, real estate educational institution or a program sponsored by a real estate association). The courses may be taken by correspondence or other distance learning instruction.

Four of the eight hours must cover the subjects of fair housing laws, state real estate laws and regulations, and ethics and standards of conduct. The remaining four hours may be on any approved subject. Nonresident licensees may substitute continuing education completed in their jurisdiction for the remaining four hours. The approved subjects include

- property rights
- contracts
- deeds
- mortgages and deeds of trust
- types of mortgages
- leases
- liens
- real property and title insurance
- investment
- taxes in real estate
- real estate financing
- brokerage and agency contract responsibilities
- real property management
- search, examination and registration of title
- title closing
- appraisal of real property
- planning subdivision developments and condominiums
- regulatory statutes
- housing legislation
- fair housing
- REB regulations
- land use
- business law
- real estate economics
- real estate investments
- federal real estate law
- commercial real estate
- Americans with Disabilities Act
- environmental issues impacting real estate
- building codes and design
- local laws and zoning ordinances
- escrow requirements
- ethics and standards of conduct

The REB may approve other subjects as well.

Licensees are responsible for retaining for three years and providing proof of continuing education. A certificate of course completion issued by the school and containing the hours of credit completed is adequate proof of course completion. Failure by the licensee to provide a course completion certification as directed by the board will result in the license not being renewed and, possibly, disciplinary action.

The REB requires each school to establish and maintain a record of continuing education for each student for a minimum of five years.

Any person who is *active* at the time of license renewal must complete the required course or courses as a condition of renewal. The courses *must* be completed prior to the date the license expires. An active licensee who does not complete the continuing education requirement prior to license expiration may complete the courses during the period of time allowed for license reinstatement (one year) but cannot reinstate the license until the continuing education course is completed.

Any person who is *inactive* at the time of license renewal may renew his or her inactive license and is *not* required to complete the course as a condition of renewal. However, when that licensee chooses to activate the license, he or she must document that the required continuing education course has been completed within the past 24 months.

Referral agents are considered active and therefore must complete the course as a condition of renewal.

EXEMPTIONS FROM LICENSURE [LL §54.1-2103]

The law recognizes that under certain circumstances, individuals or business operations engaging in what could be considered an act of real estate brokerage may be entitled to exemption from the requirements of licensure. Those conditions include, but are not limited to, the following:

- Owners, lessors and their employees dealing with their own property

- Persons acting as attorneys-in-fact under a power of attorney for final consummation of contracts for sale, lease or exchange of real estate

- Attorneys-at-law in the performance of duties as an attorney-at-law, to include the sale of real estate, condemnation proceedings and so forth

- Receivers, trustees in bankruptcy, administrators, executors or other persons acting under court order

- Trustees under trust agreements, deeds of trust or wills, or their employees

- Corporations managing rental housing when officers, directors and members in the ownership corporation and the management corporation are the same persons and the management corporation manages no property for others

- Any existing tenant of a residential dwelling who refers a prospective tenant to the owner of the unit or to the owner's agent or employee and receives, or is offered, a referral fee from the owner, agent or employee

- Auctioneers when selling real estate at public auction when employed by the owner (an auctioneer cannot advertise that he or she is authorized to sell real estate)

- Salaried residential property managers

- Appraisers, mortgage bankers and loan officers in the normal practice of their profession

All real estate licensees are always required to comply with the REB regulations, even though they also may be in one of the exempt categories.

Rental Location Agents

Rental location agents provide a service to the real estate industry but are not required to maintain a real estate license. Rental location agents are no longer regulated.

A rental location agent is defined as any person who provides rental information to prospective tenants, assists or attempts to assist, or offers to assist any person to rent or lease real property owned by another. The rental location agent may collect a fee for this service. Rental location agents also accept listings from owners or managers in expectation of compensation by including their property in information offered to prospective tenants. A rental location agent does *not* negotiate leases or offer to sell or offer

information about property for sale. The agents only refer prospective tenants to property.

License, Renewal and Registration Fees

The statute allows for the collection of fees associated with the issuance and renewal of licenses. The REB has the authority to set these charges. The purpose of these fees is to help defray the cost of administering the license law and to fund services provided by the REB to the real estate community throughout Virginia. (The current fee structure is shown in Figure 10.1)

OBTAINING A LICENSE

Once a license applicant has successfully completed the educational requirements, the next step is to take and pass an examination administered by the REB or a designated testing service. In Virginia, real estate licensing examinations are prepared by the PSI Real Estate Licensing Examination Service.

An examination application is provided by the educational provider, who certifies that the applicant has successfully met the educational requirements prescribed by the REB. The applicant makes an appointment to take the examination, which is offered each weekday.

The examination is administered by computer, and applicants will know the results as soon as they have completed the exam. Later, the applicant will receive written confirmation of having successfully passed the examination. The written notice is used as part of the application for licensure. New license applicants may have their licenses issued as either active or inactive.

Figure 10.1   Current Licensing Fees [18 VAC 135-20-80; 135-20-120]

Salesperson	
By education and examination	$90.00
Initial license by reciprocity	75.00
Renewals	46.00
Individual License - Business Entity	90.00
Renewals	46.00
Brokers	
By education and examination	100.00
Initial license by reciprocity	100.00
Renewal	50.00
Concurrent license	90.00
Renewal of concurrent license	50.00
Firms	
Initial application	145.00
Renewal	75.00
Branch Offices	
Initial application	75.00
Renewal	45.00
Application to transfer	35.00
To activate an inactive license	35.00
Reinstatement of expired license	100.00
Examination Fees	
Registration, brokers and salespersons	68.50
Phone or fax registration, additional fee	5.00
Bad check penalty	25.00

Note: These fees are subject to change at any time. Fees are for licensure only and do not include assessments to the Transaction Recovery Fund. License fees are nonrefundable.

BROKERAGES [18 VAC 135-20-160 through 135-20-170]

There may be only *one* principal broker for each firm, regardless of the number of agents affiliated with that firm or the number of offices the firm operates.

Name of Business

A brokerage business may be known by any name that identifies the owner or owners, or it may use an assumed or fictitious name. If the firm chooses to operate under an assumed or fictitious name, the application for licensure of the firm must be accompanied by a certificate of ownership that has been filed with the clerk of the court in the jurisdiction in which the business operates. This fictitious or assumed name is the name by which the business will be known to the public.

Place of Business

Every licensed broker who is a resident of Virginia must maintain a place of business within the Commonwealth. A *place of business* is defined as one where the business of real estate brokerage is normally transacted and where business calls can be directed and received. A place of business may be located in a private residence only if the business area is separate and distinct from the living quarters and is accessible to the public.

Branch Offices

If a broker operates more than one office in Virginia, the broker shall designate one location to be the main office and all other locations will be designated as branch offices.

A separate license is required for each branch office. The branch office license application shall indicate the name of the brokerage, the address of the branch office and the name of the supervising broker for that particular office.

Each place of business, including branch offices, must be supervised and personally managed by an on-premises broker who is in the office or easily accessible during normal business hours. Only the principal broker or an associate broker may be designated to manage an office and the designated person may manage only one office.

Signage

The broker may display a sign at his or her offices. Any sign must state the name by which the brokerage is known to the public (that is, the name that appears on the license issued by the REB) and the words *Real Estate*, *Realty* or the name of a generally recognized organization of real estate professionals. The signs must indicate clearly that the business being conducted is real estate brokerage.

Control of Licenses

Every principal broker must display the firm's license, the principle broker's license and the license of each salesperson and broker associated with the firm. The licenses must be displayed in the main office of the brokerage.

The only license that should be on display in any branch office is the branch office license. In addition, a roster of every salesperson and broker assigned to the branch office must be displayed in the branch office location.

Change of Location, Name or Ownership

In the event the broker's main office changes location, or the name of the brokerage changes, it is the principal broker's responsibility to advise the REB of the change within ten days. The REB will issue new licenses for the remainder of the license period. This is necessary because the broker's name and business address appear on individual licenses.

If the location of a branch office changes, only the branch office license needs to be returned.

Salespersons and individual brokers are responsible for keeping the REB informed of their current home addresses and of any changes in their name or address within 30 days of the change.

Transfer and Termination of Affiliation

If the licensee transfers from one broker to another, it is the responsibility of the licensee, along with the new broker, to make proper application to the REB to effect the transfer and have a new license issued.

Upon receipt of an application to transfer, the REB notifies the former broker of the request. If the old license has not been previously returned, the former broker must return it within ten days of the REB's notice.

The REB has ruled that if a current licensee transfers from one broker to another, the licensee may begin working for the new broker as soon as the new broker and the licensee mail the transfer application to the REB.

The individual license is never sent from one broker to another or given to the licensee to deliver to another broker because licenses must be maintained in the control of the principal broker at all times. A license travels only between the REB and the employing broker.

Any time that a salesperson or associate broker terminates affiliation with a particular firm, it is the responsibility of the principal broker of the firm to return the license of that individual to the REB.

The broker shall note on the face of the license the date of termination and shall sign the license and send it to the REB, by certified mail, to ensure receipt within ten days following the termination. The broker is also required to return the license of any person changing from active to inactive status. By definition, inactive means that the licensee is not affiliated with any brokerage firm or sole proprietor.

On termination of affiliation, the broker *must* return the individual license to the REB, regardless of the reason for termination.

Disclosure by Licensee

A licensee must disclose, in writing, his or her position and license status when acquiring or disposing of any interest in real property for any of the following:

* Himself or herself

* Immediate family members

* Members of his or her firm

- Any entity in which he or she has an ownership interest

This disclosure applies to all licensees, regardless of whether the licensee's status is active or inactive.

BROKER ESCROW ACCOUNTS
[LL §54.1-2108; 18 VAC 135-20-180]

Any broker who holds money belonging to others pending consummation or termination of a real estate transaction must maintain an escrow account solely for those funds. There is, however, no requirement that a broker hold a buyer's earnest money deposit, for instance, prior to closing. The money may be held by a settlement agent, an attorney or even the seller. Who holds the earnest money deposit is a matter to be negotiated in the sales contract. Other funds that require an escrow account include down payments, rental payments and security deposits. If a fund is to be deposited in an escrow account, it must be deposited by the fifth business banking day following ratification (sale) or receipt (lease), unless otherwise agreed in writing.

Establishing and Maintaining an Escrow Account

Each account established shall be opened and maintained in a federally insured depository in Virginia. When the account is opened, it must be made clear to the financial institution that the account is an escrow account. Each account — and all checks, deposit slips and bank statements relating to it — must be labeled *Escrow* as part of the account name. The designation of the account as an escrow account precludes attachment of the funds by the broker's creditors. It also puts the financial institution on notice that this account contains funds that belong to people other than the broker who opened the account.

The principal broker will, and the supervising broker may, be held responsible for these accounts. Individual salespersons and associate brokers do *not* have escrow accounts.

Once deposited, no funds may be removed from the escrow account until the transaction is consummated unless agreed to, in writing, by all principals to the transaction. In the event that the transaction is not consummated, the broker or supervising broker shall hold funds in escrow until one of the following events occurs:

- All principals to the transaction agree, in writing, to the disposition,

- A court orders disbursement, or

- The broker can determine, in accordance with the specific terms of the contract, exactly who is the rightful recipient of the funds

If the broker makes the determination of how funds will be distributed in accordance with the contract, the principal or supervising broker must advise each principal concerning the intended distribution. Notice of distribution must be given in writing and hand-delivered or sent by regular and certified mail to ensure that it is received. The notice advises the parties of the intended distribution and states that unless a written protest is received by the broker within 30 days, the funds will be distributed as outlined in the notice. If the principals cannot agree, the broker must petition the court to step in and decide how the money should be disbursed.

If escrow funds are used to purchase a certificate of deposit, the pledging or hypothecation of the certificate or the absence of the original from the direct control of the principal or supervising broker constitutes commingling.

Any money in the escrow account that will ultimately belong to the broker may be left in the account and not be considered commingling, provided that these funds are clearly identified in the account records and that these funds are removed from the account at periodic intervals of not more than six months. Withdrawals from the escrow account for payment of commissions shall be paid to the firm by a check drawn on the escrow account.

If necessary, the broker may use a nominal amount of personal funds to establish or maintain the escrow account and not be guilty of commingling, provided that any funds so used are clearly identified in the account records.

Interest-Bearing Accounts

There is no legal requirement that escrow funds be held in an interest-bearing account. If the escrow account does earn interest, the broker must disclose, in writing, to all parties involved exactly how any interest earned will be disbursed. Such disclosure shall be made at the time the contract or lease is written.

Property Management

Brokers acting as property managers need to maintain escrow accounts. They will be receiving monies as security deposits that will

ultimately be returned to tenants. They also receive rental money that belongs to the property owner. Brokers who manage several different properties should establish separate accounts for each property, even if the properties are owned by the same person. A broker cannot use funds from one property for another or disburse monies from an escrow or property management escrow account unless there is sufficient money on deposit in the account.

Financial Records

The broker must maintain a bookkeeping system that accurately and clearly discloses full compliance with the requirements of these regulations. The records must include the following information:

- The source of the funds
- The date the funds were received
- The date the funds were deposited
- Where the funds were deposited
- The date money was disbursed from the account
- The name of the person or persons who received the money

Escrow account records must be maintained for three years from date of consummation or termination of the transaction.

Protection of Escrow Funds

The mismanagement of escrow funds is the basis of many complaints filed with the REB. If the Board has reason to believe that a broker is unable to properly protect escrow funds, for whatever reason, it may petition the court to intercede. The court may bar the licensee from any further activity with the escrow account and take whatever other actions are necessary to protect the funds. The court may appoint a receiver to manage the funds, pending a complete investigation by the REB. It is the court that makes the appointment, not the Real Estate Board.

If, as a result of the investigation, it is determined that the licensee has been at fault or mismanaged the escrow funds, he or she must pay the costs of the receiver. If the licensee has no funds to pay the receiver, the receiver will be paid from any monies in the escrow account that would normally be due the licensee. If no such funds are available, the receiver will be paid from the Transaction Recovery Fund.

If the investigation determines that the licensee is not at fault, the receiver will be paid from the funds of the REB.

ADVERTISING [18 VAC 135-20-190]

REB regulations define *advertising* to be any oral or written communication between a licensee and anyone else. Advertising includes telephone communications, insignias, business cards, telephone directory listings, listing agreements, contracts of sale, billboards, signs, letterheads, and radio, television, magazines, newspapers and Internet advertisements.

All advertising must be under the direct supervision and control of the principal broker or supervising broker.

Any ad must indicate, affirmatively and unmistakably, that the advertising party is a real estate broker. There can be no suggestion or implication that the property being advertised is "for sale by owner." The name of the firm, as it is known to the public, must appear in every ad. The name of the brokerage must be clear and legible.

No advertisement may be published in which only a post office box, phone number or street address appears. People responding to the ad must know they are dealing with a real estate broker.

If a licensee is selling property that he or she owns, or in which he or she has an ownership interest, all advertisements must disclose the fact that the owner is licensed, unless the property is listed with a recognized real estate entity. This disclosure cannot imply that the licensee is operating a real estate brokerage business. It must be clear in the advertisement that a real estate entity is involved in the transaction.

Institutional and Noninstitutional Advertising

Institutional advertising is an advertisement in which no specific licensee or property is identified. Rather, a logo or service mark (owned by an entity other than the licensee) is used. This type of advertising is generally associated with franchise-type brokerage organizations, but it may be used by independent firms as well. The ad must clearly state that the services offered are those of real estate brokerage.

If a broker of a franchise office uses the same type of ad, the ad also requires a statement that the office is independently owned and operated. This disclosure is required in radio, television, newspaper, telephone directory and oral advertising. However, the disclosure is not required for noninstitutional advertising such as:

- telephone calls;
- signs located on a specific property for sale or rent;
- ads for a single, specific property containing no more than 28 lines; or
- single-line, one-column telephone directory ads.

However, in oral noninstitutional advertising, the licensee's name must be disclosed. In communications other than telephone conversations, the independent ownership and operation of the firm or sole proprietorship must be disclosed.

FOR EXAMPLE . . .

ABC Realty Franchise places an advertisement in the local newspaper. Because this is an institutional advertisement, it displays the ABC Realty logo, a photo of a single-family home and the message, "List your home today with an ABC Realty broker!"

Marianne Smith, an ABC Realty broker, decides to use this same advertisement as a mailing to attract new business. In order to comply with the advertising regulations, Marianne must also list her name and disclose that her office is independently owned and operated.

DEATH OR DISABILITY [LL §54.1-2109]

If a sole proprietor or the only broker in a firm dies or becomes disabled, the REB may authorize an unlicensed individual to conclude the broker's business. The individual appointed may be an adult member of the broker's family; an employee of the broker or some other suitable person. The person appointed may act only to conclude the business of the broker and may act in this capacity for a period of not longer than 180 days.

If the deceased was a sole proprietor or the only broker in the firm, two things happen by operation of law:

1. All listings are terminated.

2. The licenses of any licensees affiliated with the broker or firm must be returned to the REB since there is no longer a broker to be responsible for licensees, who are not allowed to operate in their own names.

If the principal broker of a large real estate firm dies, the officers of the firm designate a new principal broker and immediately communicate that information to the REB.

THE VIRGINIA REAL ESTATE TRANSACTION RECOVERY FUND [LL §54.1-2112 et seq.]

Purpose of the Fund

The Virginia Real Estate Transaction Recovery Fund was established for the purpose of reimbursing parties who suffer monetary loss due to a licensee's improper or dishonest conduct.

Maintenance of the Fund

The establishment and maintenance of the fund is the duty of the Director of the Department of

Professional and Occupational Regulation. The cost of administering the fund is paid out of interest earned on deposits. The REB may, at its discretion, use part of the interest earned by the fund for research and education for the benefit of licensees.

Each new licensee, whether salesperson or broker, must pay $20 into the fund. Monies collected must be deposited into the fund within 30 days after receipt by the director.

The funds's minimum balance is $400,000. If the balance of the fund falls below $400,000 the REB may assess each active and inactive licensee a proportionate amount to bring the balance to the statutory minimum. No licensee may be assessed more than $20 during any two-year period ending on June 30 of even-numbered years. Licensees who fail to pay the assessment within 45 days of receiving the first notice are given a second notice. Failure to pay the assessment within 30 days of the second notice results in automatic suspension of the licensee's license. The license will be suspended until such time as the director receives the amount due. The REB has the power to assess all licensees at one time or upon individual licensees' renewals.

At the close of each fiscal year, if the balance of the Fund is more than $2 million, the excess amount over $2 million is transferred to the Virginia Housing Partnership Fund.

Claims Procedure

A person who files a claim for payment from the fund must first obtain a judgment against the licensee from a Virginia court of competent authority. After a licensee has been found guilty of misconduct, the injured party must take appropriate legal action against the licensee. Appropriate legal action includes

- forcing the sale of the licensee's assets to satisfy all or part of the claim;

- investigating any listings held by the licensee and determine any commissions that may be due;

- filing a claim in bankruptcy court, if the licensee has filed bankruptcy; and

- requiring the licensee to submit to interrogatories, if necessary.

If any portion of the claim remains unsatisfied, the individual may file a claim with the REB requesting payment from the fund for the unsatisfied portion of the claim within 12 months from the date of the final judgment.

The claim must be accompanied by an affidavit stating the licensee's improper conduct, and the actions taken to recover damages from sources other than the fund.

A claimant must have pursued all legal means for possible recovery before a claim can be filed with the REB. On receipt of a claim, the REB will promptly consider the request and notify the claimant, in writing, of its findings.

Limitation on Recovery

No payment will be made to any of the following:

- Any licensee or a licensee's personal representative

- The spouse or child of any licensee against whom the judgment was awarded, or their personal representative

- Any financial or lending institution

- Any person whose business involves the construction or development of real property

The claim can be only for the difference between the original loss and any amount previously recovered through the legal process associated with the final judgment.

The amount of the claim is limited to actual monetary damages suffered in the transaction, court costs and attorney's fees. The claim cannot include interest, punitive or exemplary damages, even though these amounts may have been included in the judgment awarded by the court.

Funds Available

If at any time the amount of claims to be paid from the fund would deplete the fund to an amount below the statutory minimum ($400,000), the processing of all claims will be suspended. The REB will assess regulants as previously outlined. As funds become available to satisfy the pending claims, they will be paid in the order in which they were originally received.

In all cases, the REB may withhold payment of any claim for 12 months if it has reason to believe that additional claims may be filed. In the event there are multiple claims against a licensee that exceed the maximum allowable

payment from the fund, each claimant will receive a proportionate share of the total payment.

Monetary Limitations on Claims

Single Transaction. In a single transaction, the maximum payment from the fund to all injured parties is $50,000. The maximum amount any single claimant may recover from the fund based on a single transaction is $20,000, regardless of the number of claimants.

Multiple Transactions. If the same licensee is involved in multiple fraudulent transactions during any two-year period ending June 30 of even-numbered years, the maximum payment to all claimants combined is $100,000.

If a payment is made from the fund, the claimant must *subrogate* his or her rights to the REB. Subrogation permits the REB to take action against the licensee to recover the amount of claims paid due to the licensee's misconduct.

Penalty

Payment from the fund causes the licensee's license to be *immediately revoked.* The respondent may also be subject to other disciplinary action by the REB. The licensee may not apply for a new license until the fund has been repaid in full, plus interest at the judgment rate of interest from the date of payment from the fund.

Repayment of the fund does not guarantee that the license will be reissued. The REB may take disciplinary action against a licensee for a disciplinable violation regardless of whether or not he or she has reimbursed the fund.

STANDARDS OF CONDUCT

The regulations promulgated by the REB establish certain required standards of professional behavior expected of all real estate licensees in Virginia.

Disclosure of Interest
[18 VAC 135-20-210]

If a licensee has any family, business or financial relationship with any of the principals to the contract, all parties to the contract must be informed, in writing in the offer to purchase or lease, of the relationship. This requirement applies to any licensee who could be considered an "interested party" to the transaction.

Disclosure of Brokerage Relationships and Dual or Designated Agency
[18 VAC 135-20-220]

Unless disclosure has been made previously, a licensee must disclose to an actual or prospective buyer or seller who is not the client of the licensee and who is not represented by another licensee the party he or she represents. In the case of both buyers and sellers, the disclosure must be made when "substantive discussions about specific property" take place. The disclosure must be provided "at the earliest practical time, but in no event later than the time specific real estate assistance is first provided."

The disclosure must advise prospective buyers, sellers, landlords or tenants of the duties of real estate brokers and salespersons under Virginia law, and encourage them to obtain relevant information from other sources.

A licensee who is acting as a dual or designated representative must obtain the written consent of all parties "at the earliest practical time." The disclosure may be made in conjunction with other required disclosures if it is conspicuous, printed in bold lettering, all capitals, underlined or within a separate box.

IN PRACTICE . . .
The REB's regulations do not contain a list of specific events that trigger the disclosure requirement. Common sense should tell the licensee when disclosure is required: if in doubt, disclose.

Licensees Dealing on Own Account
[18 VAC 135-20-230]

Licensees may — and many do — sell or lease property that they personally own. Years of training, experience and expertise give a licensee particular effectiveness as a FSBO ("*fizz-boe*" is an acronym for "For Sale By Owner"). Some licensees feel that there is no point in paying a broker's commission to someone else to do what they can do perfectly well themselves. While permissible, licensees who engage in transactions on their own are still bound by the rules and regulations of the REB in the same manner as if they were representing a client in a professional capacity.

Provision of Records to the Board
[18 VAC 135-20-240]

The REB has the authority to audit a broker's transaction records. Records must be kept for three years following consummation or termination of a transaction. Licensees must respond to any inquiry from the REB within 21 days.

Unworthiness and Incompetence [18 VAC 135-20-260]

Actions that constitute unworthy and incompetent conduct include

- obtaining a license by false or fraudulent representation — for instance, providing false information in the license application or cheating on the license examination. It is also improper for a currently licensed real estate salesperson to sit for the salesperson's licensing examination, or a currently licensed broker to sit for the broker's examination (of course, a qualified, licensed salesperson may sit for the broker's exam);

- holding more than one license as a real estate broker or salesperson in Virginia, unless permitted to do so by law. Only brokers may hold more than one Virginia license.

- having been finally convicted or found guilty of a misdemeanor involving moral turpitude, sexual offense, drug distribution or physical injury, or any felony. Any plea of nolo contendere is considered a conviction. Just as an individual can be denied a license because of past criminal convictions, a license can be taken away on the same basis.

- failing to inform the board in writing within 30 days of pleading guilty or nolo contendere or being convicted or found guilty of any felony or of a misdemeanor involving moral turpitude, sexual offense, drug distribution or physical injury;

- having been found guilty of violating the Virginia Fair Housing Act or any other local, state or federal fair housing laws; and

- failing to act in such a manner as to safeguard the interests of the public, or otherwise engaging in improper, fraudulent, or dishonest conduct.

Conflict of Interest [18 VAC 135-20-270]

Actions constituting a conflict of interest include

- being employed by, affiliated with or receiving compensation from a real estate broker other than the licensee's principal broker, without the written consent of the principal broker;

- acting for more than one party in a transaction without the written consent of all principals for whom the licensee acts. Dual agency is not illegal in Virginia, provided that the principals to the transaction know about it and agree to it in writing.

- acting as a standard agent or independent contractor for any client in a real estate transaction outside the licensee's brokerage firm or sole proprietorship. All of a licensee's, salesperson's or associate broker's acts of real estate brokerage must be conducted in the name of the employing broker.

Improper Brokerage Commission
[18 VAC 135-20-280]

Brokers may pay commissions or fees to any licensees affiliated with their firm. Brokers also may pay commissions or fees to other brokers (or firms), regardless of where those brokers are located.

Salespersons and associate brokers may only receive compensation from the broker whose name appears on their licenses.

If commissions are earned but not paid during the period of employment or affiliation with a broker, the previous broker may pay the licensee directly, even though the licensee may be affiliated with another broker or no longer actively licensed.

Licensees are barred from receiving kickbacks from a third party who provides services or goods necessary to fulfill a contract (such as an appraiser, home inspector, or surveyor), when one of the principals to the contract is paying for the services. The principals must be informed, in writing, of any "finder's fees" or commissions paid to the licensee.

Similarly, a licensee may not personally pay for services required by the terms of a real estate contract without written disclosure of the payment to the principals. For instance, a buyer might be short of the cash needed to pay for a survey of the property. If the licensee agrees to pay for the survey personally, there could be accusations later that the survey was inferior or not done by a competent professional surveyor unless the principals agree to the arrangement. The licensee has a personal interest in the transaction being completed; offering to pay for

one of the steps necessary for completion could appear to be self-serving.

Net listings are not permitted in Virginia.

Finally, no licensee may charge money or other valuable consideration to, or accept or receive money or valuable consideration from, any person or entity *other than the licensee's principal* for expenditures made on the principal's behalf without the written consent of the principal.

Improper Dealing [18 VAC 135-20-290]

Actions that constitute improper dealing include

- entering into a brokerage relationship that does not have a specific, definite termination date. Most listing and buyer representation agreements include a blank space in which the date may be inserted.

- offering property for sale or lease without the owner's knowledge and consent, or on terms other than those authorized by the owner.

- placing *any* sign on *any* property without permission. This regulation could include the placement of directional signs on the property of someone other than the seller.

- advertising property for sale, rent, or lease in any newspaper, periodical, or sign without including in the advertisement the name of the firm or sole proprietorship.

Misrepresentations and Omissions [18 VAC 135-20-300]

The regulations prohibit specific actions as misrepresentations or omissions. They are:

- using "bait and switch" tactics by advertising or offering real property for sale or rent with the intent not to sell or rent at the price or terms advertised, unless the advertisement or offer clearly states that the property advertised is limited in specific quantity and the licensee or registrant did in fact have at least that quantity for sale or rent.

- failing to disclose material information related to the property that is reasonably available to the licensee. A dual representative may not disclose confidential information to either client.

- failing to promptly present *every* written offer, rejection or counteroffer to the buyer and seller.

- failing to include the *complete* terms and conditions of the real estate transaction in any offer to purchase or rent, including identification of all those holding any deposits.

- knowingly making any false statement or report, or willfully misstating the value of any land, property, or security for the purpose of influencing a lender regarding applications, advance discounts, purchase agreements, repurchase agreements, commitments of loans, or to change the terms or time limits of a loan.

- making *any* misrepresentation.

- making a false promise through agents, salespersons, advertising, or other means.

Delivery of Instruments [18 VAC 135-20-310]

Actions constituting improper delivery of instruments include

- failing to promptly deliver complete and legible copies of any written listings, offers to lease, offers to purchase, counteroffers, addenda and ratified agreements to each party in a transaction: anyone who signs his or her name to a document is entitled to a copy;

- failing to provide timely, written notice of any material change in the transaction to all parties;

- failing to deliver a complete and accurate statement of money received and disbursed by the licensee, duly signed and certified by the principal or supervising broker (or his or her authorized agent), to the seller and buyer at the time a real estate transaction is completed. However, if the transaction is closed by a settlement agent other than the licensee (or his or her broker), and if the financial disclosure is provided on the applicable settlement statement, the licensee is not required to provide a separate statement of receipts and disbursements.

- refusing or failing without just cause to surrender any document or instrument to the rightful owner upon demand.

Recordkeeping and Escrow Funds
[18 VAC 135-20-320]

The regulations provide for the manner in which financial and transaction records are to be kept and escrow funds maintained.

Actions that constitute improper record keeping and maintenance of escrow funds include

- failing to retain a complete and legible copy of each disclosure of a brokerage relationship, executed contract, agreement, notice, closing statement and other material documents related to a real estate transaction in the broker's control or possession for a period of three years from the date of the closing;

- failing to maintain, for a period of three years from the date of the closing, a complete and accurate record of monies received and disbursed on behalf of others;

- failing to account for or remit, within a reasonable time, any funds coming into a licensee's possession that belong to others;

- accepting any note, nonnegotiable instrument (such as a promissory note or postdated check), or anything of value not readily negotiable, as a deposit on a contract, offer to purchase, or lease, without acknowledging its acceptance in the agreement;

- commingling any person's funds with the personal or business funds of a principal or supervising broker or his or her employees, associates, corporation, firm, or association, or failing to deposit those funds in an account designated to receive only those funds as required by Virginia law (that is, escrow accounts).

Principal and Supervising Broker's Responsibility for Licensees
[18 VAC 135-20-330]

A principal or supervising broker is liable for the unlawful acts of a real estate salesperson, employee, partner or affiliate of a principal or supervising broker only if the REB finds that the principal or supervising broker knew or should have known of the unlawful act or violation.

Effect of Disciplinary Action on Subordinate Licensees
[18 VAC 315-20-340]

If a principal broker's or sole proprietor's license is revoked or suspended, or if renewal is denied, the licenses of any and all individuals affiliated with or employed by the affected firm are automatically ordered returned to the REB until such time as they are reissued upon the written request of another sole proprietor or principal broker. That is, affiliated licensees must either transfer or become inactive.

COMPLAINT PROCEDURE

The REB has the authority to investigate the activities of any licensee. The REB usually investigates as a result of a written complaint, but it does have the authority to start an investigation on its own initiative.

A complaint must be in writing, supported by documentary evidence that clearly demonstrates that the accused licensee's actions violate the law. The REB reviews the complaint first, to determine if the actions described are within its scope of authority. If not, the complaint is referred to the proper regulatory authority or returned to the complainant.

All complaints must be filed within three years of the transaction date or, in specific situations, within two years of discovery.

If it is determined that the complaint should be investigated, the named licensee and his or her principal broker is notified. The REB recognizes that a person is innocent until proven guilty and is entitled to have his or her day in court before any sanctions are imposed. All proceedings are conducted in accordance with the Administrative Process Act, Title 9, Chapter 1.1.1 of the Code of Virginia.

An investigator from the Enforcement Bureau of the Department of Professional and Occupational Regulation interviews the complainant, the accused licensee, and witnesses. The investigator's findings are reported to the REB without comment or recommendation. The REB then reviews the investigator's report. The case may be dismissed if the REB feels that no violation occurred.

If the REB finds that a violation has occurred, the licensee is given an opportunity to admit guilt and settle the matter through a consent order. The licensee agrees to refrain from the wrongful act, promises not to do it again, and agrees to accept whatever sanctions are imposed by the REB. A respondent who does not agree

to the consent order may request an Informal Fact Finding Conference (IFFC).

The IFFC is presided over by a member of the REB, who hears testimony of the respondent, claimant and witnesses. Based on the testimony, the REB member either recommends that the case be dismissed or allows the respondent to admit guilt and enter a consent order. The final decision to accept either option requires ratification by the full REB membership.

If a consent order is not agreed to, the matter is referred to a formal hearing conducted by a hearing officer appointed by the Virginia Supreme Court. An assistant attorney general is assigned to present the facts and argue the case that a violation has been committed. The hearing officer reports to the REB and states his or her conclusions, based strictly on the law. The hearing officer does not recommend sanctions. After a review of the hearing officer's report, the REB either closes the case or cites the violations and imposes sanctions.

If the REB finds the licensee guilty, it may impose a monetary penalty of up to $1,000 for each violation. The REB may also suspend, revoke or deny renewal of the respondent's license. The REB's decision is final, although the licensee may appeal the decision through the Court of Appeals. In all of these proceedings, the accused has the right to be represented by legal counsel.

Automatic License Suspension or Revocation

There are two instances in which disciplinary action may be taken against a licensee, and his or her license may be suspended or revoked without review or a hearing:

1. If a licensee does not pay the assessment to the Transaction Recovery Fund, his or her license will be automatically *suspended*.

2. If a payment is made from the Transaction Recovery Fund, the license of the respondent will be automatically *revoked*.

Questions

1. A broker's business is growing, and now she wants to open a branch office. Which of the following is true?

   a. The office must have an escrow account.
   b. The office may be managed by a salesperson with three years of experience.
   c. The office must have a separate license.
   d. The branch office will display the licenses of all salespersons and associate brokers assigned to that particular office.

2. A salesperson decides to retire. When the salesperson terminates his or her affiliation, what must he or she do?

   a. Give the broker an official letter of termination that he or she can send to the REB.
   b. Nothing; the broker is responsible for notifying the REB of the change.
   c. Return all customer cards to the employing broker.
   d. Return his or her license, along with a letter of termination, to the REB.

3. A licensee who allows his or her license to expire has how long to reinstate the license without monetary penalty?

   a. Up to 15 days
   b. Up to 30 days
   c. No more than 365 days
   d. One year from the last June 23

4. Yore Realty opens its first office in Richmond. Which of the following is a permissible sign to place in front of the office?

   a. "*YORE OFFICE*"
   b. "*YORE HOUSE: We Serve Richmond's Homeowners*"
   c. "*YORE REALTY*"
   d. "*YORE: A Member of the Greater Richmond Chamber of Commerce*"

5. Is it possible to become licensed in Virginia without taking the Virginia real estate license examination?

   a. No
   b. Yes, if the person is licensed to practice law in Virginia
   c. Yes, because any person who is currently licensed in another jurisdiction and meets all requirements for reciprocity may be licensed in Virginia
   d. Yes, if the person is an appraiser

6. Which of the following is an accurate description of the Real Estate Board?

   a. Seven members; six licensees and one consumer
   b. Seven members; five licensees and two consumers
   c. Nine members; either licensed brokers or salespersons
   d. Nine members; seven licensees and two consumers

7. A licensed salesperson may hold a concurrent license with more than one Virginia broker under which of the following circumstances?

   a. Under no circumstances
   b. With the permission of his or her sales manager
   c. With the written consent of the brokers being represented
   d. With the permission of the REB

8. Every Virginia real estate office is required to

   a. maintain escrow account records for five years.
   b. keep transaction records for three years.
   c. display signage at the office location.
   d. employ at least one salesperson.

9. A licensee was out of town on vacation. When she returned on October 10, she found her license renewal notice and realized that her license had expired on July 31. If she wants to remain licensed, she must

   a. reapply for a new license as a new applicant.
   b. meet the current educational requirements.
   c. apply for reinstatement of her license and pay $100.
   d. apply to have her license placed on inactive status.

10. All of the following statements are correct regarding an active licensed broker who has been licensed in Virginia since 1975, *EXCEPT*

    a. the broker may be licensed in more than one legal real estate entity.
    b. the broker is exempt from the continuing education requirements on the basis of having been licensed for more than 15 years.
    c. the broker may contract to be a property manager.
    d. the broker's office may be located in his or her home under certain circumstances.

11. What must appear on all "For Sale" signs placed on property by a broker?

    a. The broker's phone number
    b. The name of the person who listed the property
    c. The selling price of the property
    d. The name of the broker

12. What is the minimum balance of the Virginia Real Estate Transaction Recovery Fund?

    a. $800,000   c. $600,000
    b. $750,000   d. $400,000

13. How often are real estate licenses renewed in Virginia?

    a. Annually, in the month issued
    b. Every two years, in the month of the licensee's birthday
    c. On June 30 of each even-numbered year
    d. Biennially, in the month issued

14. When a salesperson is alleged to have violated the license law, possibly resulting in disciplinary action, which of the following statements is true?

   a. An investigation will be conducted by the REB.
   b. The salesperson is entitled to a jury trial before any action can be taken.
   c. The salesperson's license will be temporarily suspended until the Board can schedule a formal hearing.
   d. The employing broker also is charged with the same violation.

15. If a broker is holding an earnest money deposit, how long must the funds be held if the sales contract does not close?

   a. Until the buyer requests a refund
   b. Until the broker is asked for the money by an attorney representing one of the parties
   c. Until all parties to the contract agree to the intended distribution
   d. Until the broker decides it is appropriate to do so

16. A licensed salesperson is selling her own condominium and advertises it as follows: "For Sale By Owner: 3 bed. condo unit in high rise. Call 987-6543 for details. Owner licensed." Based on these facts, which of the following is true?

   a. Because the salesperson is acting in a private capacity, she is exempt from the advertising laws.
   b. The advertisement is proper because the owner has disclosed her licensee status as required by law.
   c. Virginia's advertising regulations do not apply to condominiums.
   d. The ad should have included her office number and broker.

17. Several weeks after a closing, an associate broker received a thank-you letter and a nice bonus check from the seller of the house. The associate broker cashed the check because he felt it was earned. In this situation, which of the following is true?

   a. The associate broker may accept the bonus because he is licensed as an associate broker.
   b. Accepting the money is allowed if more than 30 days have elapsed since the closing.
   c. The associate broker may accept the money if his broker permits him to do so.
   d. Accepting the money is a violation of REB regulations.

18. A broker manages three properties for the same owner. One property is in need of emergency repairs, but there is not enough money in the management account to cover the cost. The broker borrows money from the escrow account of one of the other properties to make the repairs. Which of the following is true?

   a. The broker has acted properly by safeguarding the client's interest.
   b. Such action is proper because all prop- erties are owned by the same person.
   c. The broker is in violation of regulations for improperly handling escrow funds.
   d. The broker must use personal funds for repairs if there is not enough money in the management account.

19. Under the terms of a sales contract, the seller is required to provide a termite certificate. The seller requests that the salesperson order one. The salesperson does so, knowing she will receive a referral fee from the pest control company. Is this a violation of the license law?

   a. No, if the fee is less than $25.
   b. No, if the fee is disclosed, either orally or in writing, to the parties to the contract.
   c. Yes; a salesperson may not receive a referral fee
   d. Yes; special fees may be paid to the salesperson only by the seller.

20. W, an airline pilot, told X, a broker, about some friends who were looking for a new home. X contacted the friends and eventually sold them a house. When may X pay W for the valuable lead?

   a. As soon as a valid sales contract is signed by the parties
   b. Only after the sale closes.
   c. After the funds are released from escrow
   d. X may not pay W for the lead.

21. A broker is convicted on May 1 of possession and distribution of a controlled substance. Both the crime and the conviction took place in the state of Maryland. On June 15, the broker calls the REB and leaves a message informing the REB of the conviction. Based on these facts, which of the following is true?

   a. The broker has properly informed the REB within 60 days after the conviction, and the broker's license may be renewed.
   b. Both the conviction and the broker's failure to notify the REB within 30 days violates REB regulations.
   c. Because the conviction did not occur in Virginia, it is not evidence of unworthy conduct.
   d. The conviction is evidence of both improper dealing and fraud.

22. When a salesperson takes an exclusive-right-to-sell listing, it is important that the listing agreement include all of the following information, *EXCEPT*

    a. the name of the employing broker.
    b. a definite date on which the listing will expire.
    c. an adequate property description.
    d. the net amount that the seller will receive from the sale.

23. After proper investigation, a payment is made from the Transaction Recovery Fund owing to the improper activities of *H*, a licensee. What happens when the payment is made?

    a. *H*'s license is automatically suspended.
    b. The REB takes no further action if *H* repays the fund within 30 days.
    c. *H*'s license is automatically revoked.
    d. *H* is subject to a fine of $2,000.

24. When a sole proprietor has his or her license suspended for two years, what effect does this have on the associate brokers and salespeople affiliated with the proprietor?

    a. The affiliates' licenses will be revoked, subject to reinstatement after one year.
    b. The affiliates' licenses will be also be suspended for a two-year period.
    c. The suspension has no effect on the affiliates.
    d. The affiliates' licenses must be returned to the REB.

25. A licensed salesperson obtains a listing. Several days later, the salesperson meets prospective buyers at the property and tells them, "I am the listing agent for this property, and so I'm very familiar with it." Under these circumstances, the salesperson

    a. has failed to properly disclose his or her agency relationship.
    b. has properly disclosed his or her agency relationship with the seller.
    c. is in violation of REB regulations, because the listing belongs to the broker.
    d. has created a dual agency, which is a violation of REB regulations.

26. Some ads placed by real estate franchise companies (noninstitutional advertising) must include specific disclosures. All of the following forms of advertising are exempt from the disclosure requirements *EXCEPT*

    a. one-column line listings in a telephone directory.
    b. "For Sale" yard signs on specific properties.
    c. a newspaper ad of less than 28 lines describing a single-family house.
    d. a newspaper ad of less than 28 lines describing a subdivision development.

27. If a broker establishes an account to hold money belonging to others, which of the following is correct?

    a. All checks, deposit slips and bank statements must include the word "Escrow" as part of the account name.
    b. Accounts may be labeled either "Trust" or "Escrow."
    c. The account cannot be in the same bank as the broker's personal checking account.
    d. An individual account is required for each transaction.

28. G's broker commits a fraudulent act in connection with the sale of a property on March 15, 1999. On March 30, the transaction closes. On November 1, G sues the broker, alleging fraud. On December 20, the jury finds in favor of G. When must G file a claim with REB to recover money from the Transaction Recovery Fund?

    a. The request must be filed within 30 days following the illegal activity: in this case, by April 15, 1999.
    b. Within 1 year after having been awarded a judgment by the courts: in this case, by December 20, 2000.
    c. Within 1 year of filing suit: in this case, by November 1, 2000.
    d. Within 2 years of the date of closing: in this case, by March 30, 2001.

29. Which of the following is a requirement to obtain a real estate salesperson's license in Virginia?

    a. Successful completion of 12 credit hours of real estate law, investments, finance and appraisal
    b. An associate degree or certificate in real estate from an accredited college, university or proprietary school
    c. United States and Virginia citizenship
    d. Successful completion of a course of 60 classroom, correspondence, or distance learning hours in a general principles of real estate

30. All of the following are requirements for a broker's license *EXCEPT*

    a. a college degree or certificate in business, finance, management, appraisal or real estate.
    b. 12 semester hours of designated real estate courses.
    c. three years of experience as a salesperson.
    d. not have violated Virginia's fair housing laws, or those of any other state.

11 Real Estate Financing: Principles and Practice

This chapter primarily discusses the financing of single-family residential real estate in Virginia. It does not address commercial or more sophisticated transactions, but many of the concepts addressed apply to such transactions.

PURCHASE CONTRACTS AND FINANCING

A licensed real estate broker or agent who has negotiated a sale may prepare a routine contract for the transaction. If a first deed of trust loan is to be obtained, the contract usually is made contingent on the purchaser's obtaining the loan. The real estate licensee must be careful in describing the loan because of the complexity of the terms for prevailing loans. The seller may add the provision that the purchaser must apply for the loan promptly and, should the purchaser not notify the seller by a certain date that loan approval has been obtained, the contingency shall be deemed waived. Typically, preprinted real estate contracts provide that the purchaser has five days from the date of the contract in which to apply for financing. The contract should specifically state what type of financing is contemplated: cash, assumption, seller financed, FHA, VA or conventional loan obtained through an institutional lender.

The contract should provide a ceiling on the interest rate the borrower will accept. If this condition is not included, the purchaser could be bound by the contract even if the interest rate rises several percentage points between the date the contract is ratified and the date the purchaser locks in the interest rate with a lender. The lack of an interest rate cap could end up significantly increasing the cost of the home for the buyer.

If an existing loan is to remain on the property, the contract should specify whether it will be assumed or whether title will be taken subject to the existing loan.

INSTITUTIONAL FINANCING

Conventional Loans

In Virginia, deeds of trust, rather than mortgages, are the instruments primarily used in residential sales transactions. Nearly every type of financial institution makes conventional deed of trust loans. In Virginia, the note and deed of trust give the lender the right, in the event the borrower should default, to accelerate maturity and direct the trustee to hold a nonjudicial foreclosure — a foreclosure without a court hearing — to determine the propriety of the action. By signing the note and deed of trust, the borrower waives various rights, including the court hearing. A borrower who believes the foreclosure is wrong must seek a hearing.

It is extremely important that the borrower fully understand the nature of the note and deed of trust.

The settlement attorney is normally expected to prepare any promissory note involved in the closing. Form notes are available from a variety of sources such as the VA, FHA and institutional lenders. The note is not recorded.

The note and deed of trust should be signed in the exact manner and in the same name as the title is held. No witnesses are necessary. The deed of trust must, however, be acknowledged to permit its recordation in the land records of the circuit court where the property is located. Further, VA and FHA notes, and notes to be sold out of state, require notarization.

Late Charges

Many conventional first deed of trust loans contain a provision for a late charge if a monthly payment is not made within a certain period of time after the due date (referred to as a *grace period*). The fact that a late charge may be collected must be disclosed in the loan's truth-in-lending statement. In Virginia, late charges may not exceed 5 percent of the installment due and cannot be collected unless the payment is not made within seven calendar days after the due date. Most lenders permit 15 days. The late charge must be specified in the contract between the lender and the borrower. Late charges in excess of the statutory amount are void only with regard to the excess amount; an inflated late charge does not affect the underlying obligation.

Other Charges

In addition to such charges as points, late charges and escrows, Virginia law permits lenders to charge a *loan origination fee* for granting a loan. Examples of other allowable fees are the cost of title examination, title insurance, recording charges, taxes, hazard insurance, mortgage guarantee insurance, appraisals, credit reports, surveys, document preparation, real estate tax service fees, lender inspection fees and closing the loan.

The lender generally requires a house location survey. The survey must be current (within the past six months), and the survey must be done by a certified land surveyor.

CREDIT LINE DEEDS OF TRUST

A *credit line deed of trust* permits the note holder to make advances from time to time secured by the real estate described in the deed. The total amount of advances may not exceed the maximum credit line extended to the borrower. Virginia law permits credit line deeds of trust, subject to certain rules. The trust document must identify itself as a credit line deed of trust on the front page in capital letters and underscored type. The phrase, THIS IS A CREDIT LINE DEED OF TRUST gives notice that the note holder named in the deed of trust and the grantors and other borrowers identified in the deed have an agreement.

From the date of the recording of a credit line deed of trust, the lien has priority over all other deeds, conveyances and other instruments or contracts in writing that are unrecorded at that time and of which the note holder has no knowledge. The credit line deed of trust also has priority over judgment liens subsequently docketed. However, if a judgment creditor gives notice to the note holder at the address indicated on the credit line deed of trust, the deed of trust has no priority over the judgment for any advances or extensions of credit subsequently made under the deed of trust.

DUE-ON-SALE CLAUSES

Loans that contain a due-on-sale clause (also called an alienation clause) are not assumable. Due-on-sale clauses are enforceable in Virginia.

When a loan containing a due-on-sale clause is made on real property comprising not more than four residential dwelling units, the deed of trust must contain the following language, either in capital letters or underlined:

> NOTICE — The debt secured hereby is subject to call in full or the terms thereof being modified in the event of sale or conveyance of the property conveyed.

PURCHASE-MONEY FINANCING

A deed of trust given with the conveyance of land to secure the unpaid balance of the purchase price is called a *purchase-money deed of trust*. The deed of trust should be labeled "Purchase-Money Deed of Trust." A purchase-money deed of trust has priority over all other claims or liens arising through the mortgagor, even if they are prior in time. Prior judgments against the purchaser will not come ahead of the purchase-money deed of trust. If a married purchaser takes title to the property in severalty, the spouse will not have to execute a purchase-money deed of trust.

DEFERRED PURCHASE-MONEY DEED OF TRUST

When the seller is an older person or installment sale tax treatment is desired, a deferred purchase-money deed of trust, held by the seller, is a useful method of financing. One advantage to sellers is that they usually receive a substantial down payment. Such an arrangement may be prohibited, however, if there is to be a first deed of trust to an outside (institutional) lender. A purchase-money deed of trust held by the seller should state that it is granted to secure *deferred purchase money,* while a purchase-money deed of trust to a third party states that it is granted to secure *purchase money.* If it is a second deed of trust, it can be for a short term with a balloon payment at the end. The first lender's guidelines must be followed. If it is subordinated, the purchase-money second deed of trust should include a provision that any default in a senior encumbrance or lien will also be considered a default on a second deed of trust.

RELEASES

Whenever the borrower pays off any note, a marginal release is made on the face of the instrument wherever the document is recorded. Alternatively, a certificate of satisfaction or a partial satisfaction form is filed in the deed books in the clerk's office in the county where the land is located.

VIRGINIA HOUSING DEVELOPMENT AUTHORITY

The Virginia Housing Development Authority (VHDA) extends loans to residents of the Commonwealth of Virginia under the following conditions:

- The buyer cannot have had an ownership interest in his or her primary residence during the three years prior to making the application for the loan, and all co-borrowers must be married or related.

- Private mortgage insurance is required until the loan is paid down to 80 percent of the value of the property.

- There are maximum income restrictions imposed on applicants.

- If the loan is a VHDA-VA loan, the VHDA will lend the entire purchase price and no down payment will be required to be made by the borrower with full entitlement. Other VHDA loan programs require small down payments.

- The seller must pay the single discount point.

- A power of attorney cannot be used in executing the documents; rather, both parties must personally execute all VHDA documents.

VHDA builds and operates residential housing, nursing care facilities and nursing homes. Further, the definitions of housing development, housing project and residential housing provide that medical and related facilities for the residence and care of the aged are included in the definition of "dwelling accommodation" for the purpose of the Act.

FORECLOSURE

There are three ways to foreclose a deed of trust in Virginia:

1. Decree of court (strict foreclosure)

2. Conveyance of the property by the grantors and the trustees to the beneficiary in consideration of the debt ("deed in lieu of foreclosure")

3. Sale by the trustee pursuant to a power of sale ("trustee sale")

Although an exhaustive discussion of foreclosure procedures is not necessary here, it is important for licensees to be aware that bankruptcy of the mortgagor is an automatic stay of foreclosure. If a lien is foreclosed (that is, no bankruptcy was granted), the lien and all inferior liens are wiped out. Superior liens, however — those that have priority over the foreclosed lien — are not affected. A purchaser takes the property subject to any prior liens.

VA and FHA Loans

Foreclosure of VA and FHA loans is subject to certain additional requirements. For instance, the loan must have been in default for three months prior to the commencement of foreclosure; notices must be given to both the debtor and the insuring agency; and the lender must take affirmative steps to avoid foreclosure, including personal interviews and acceptance of partial payments.

Trustee's Powers and Duties

Virginia is a *title theory* state.

Legal title to the property conveyed by the deed of trust is vested in the trustee for the benefit of the note holder. The trustee can act only in a manner authorized by statute or the express or implied terms of the trust.

The trustee is the agent for both the grantor (the homeowner) and the beneficiary (the lender) and is bound to act impartially between them. The trustee is obliged to seek every possible advantage to the trust in the course of any sale. This includes using all reasonable diligence to obtain the best price possible. The trustee may adjourn the sale from time to time to meet any unexpected occurrences, but the readvertisement of the sale must be in the same manner as the original advertisement.

If it is clear at the sale that the property will be sold for a grossly inadequate or sacrificial price, it is the trustee's duty to adjourn the sale. In addition, if the trustee knows of facts that might keep bidding low, such as a cloud on title, he or she must adjourn the sale and remove the hindrance.

By statute, the trustee must ascertain whether there are any real estate tax liens against the property being sold. The trustee is obligated to pay the taxes out of the proceeds of sale and give the tax lien priority over the deed of trust. In addition, the purchaser is required to see that the taxes are paid. If the taxes are not paid, the trustee may be liable personally and the purchaser takes the land subject to the tax lien (though not personally liable for its payment). The trustee should also pay the prorated portion of the current year's real estate taxes.

Caveat Emptor

The rule of *caveat emptor* ("let the buyer beware") applies in foreclosure sales, with regard to both the quality of title and the condition of the property.

Advertisement

The terms of the deed of trust will determine how the property is advertised. Even if the number of advertisements meets the terms, Virginia law provides that the sale may take place no earlier than the eighth day after the first advertisement and no later than 30 days after the last advertisement.

Conflict of Interest

A trustee may not purchase the property held in trust without written permission from the mortgagor. The trustee is bound by law to secure the highest possible price for the property, while a purchaser seeks to procure the property at the lowest possible price. The trustee's duty to the trust transcends any potential personal interest he or she may have or acquire in the property.

Auction

The sale must be held in accordance with the terms of the deed of trust, which specifies the time, manner and place of sale. Unless the deed of trust states otherwise, the sale is held at the property itself, or near the circuit court building, or at some other place selected by the trustee in the city or county in which the property is located.

At the sale, the trustee sells the property to the highest bidder, and the successful purchaser executes a memorandum of sale. The trustee obtains the deposit from the purchaser.

Trustee's Deed

The trustee cannot convey a greater interest than the deed of trust gives authority to sell. The sale is subject to encumbrances that have priority over the deed of trust. Accordingly, the trustee's deed should contain only a special warranty of title. However, the form of the deed and the title conveyed must conform to the manner in which the property was advertised.

Disbursement of Proceeds

The trustee must apply the proceeds of sale in the following order:

1. to discharge the *expenses of executing the trust*, including a commission to the trustee of 5 percent of the gross proceeds;

2. to *discharge all taxes, levies and assessments* with costs and interest, if they have priority over the deed of trust;

3. to discharge, in the order of their priority, any *remaining debts and obligations* secured by the deed of trust and any liens of record inferior to the deed of trust, with interest; and

4. to render the *residue of the proceeds to the grantor* (foreclosed mortgagor) or his or her assigns.

When the sale is made under any recorded deed of trust, the trustee must file a report and accounting with the commissioner of accounts within four months of the sale.

USURY

A *usurious transaction* is a contract for the loan of money at a greater rate of interest than allowed by law.

Virginia law provides that loans secured by a first deed of trust on real estate may be lawfully enforced with *no limitation on the amount of interest*, if that arrangement is properly stated in the instrument or separate agreement. The contract generally is considered to be the promissory note. Most prudent lenders insert the rate in the note.

The law provides that disclosure of charges may be contained in an interest disclosure statement if such disclosure is not otherwise specified in the note. It further provides that an interest rate that varies in accordance with any exterior standard or that cannot be ascertained from the contract without reference to exterior circumstances or documents is enforceable as agreed in the signed contract. For instance, a note providing for an interest rate of 3 percent above the stated prime rate of a specific bank would be enforceable.

Allowable Interest Rates

Where the seller in a bona fide real estate transaction takes back a purchase-money deed of trust, the promissory note may provide for *any rate of interest agreed to by the parties*. Usury is not applicable to such a transaction because the interest rate is considered a time-price differential and thus part of the purchase price.

Violation of Virginia Usury Law

Any contract, note or deed of trust made or received that provides for interest charges in excess of those permitted by Virginia law shall be null and void and unenforceable by the lender or its assignees.

WET SETTLEMENT ACT

The Wet Settlement Act applies to transactions involving purchase-money loans secured by first deeds of trust on real estate containing not more than four residential dwelling units. The act applies only to lenders regularly engaged in making loans secured by real estate.

At or before the loan closing, the lender must disburse the loan proceeds to the settlement agent. The lender may not charge or receive interest on the loan until disbursement of the loan funds and the loan closing have occurred.

The settlement agent or attorney will have the deed, deed of trust and any other necessary document recorded and will disburse the settlement proceeds within two business days of settlement. A settlement agent or attorney may not disburse any loan funds prior to recording the deed of trust or other security instrument perfecting the lender's security instrument. As a result, the seller will not receive his or her equity, and the real estate professional will not receive a commission check at the closing. Rather, all funds will be disbursed after the documents are recorded by the settlement agent.

Any person who suffers a loss because of the failure of a lender or settlement agent to disburse funds as required by law is entitled to recover double the amount of any interest collected in addition to actual damages, plus reasonable attorney's fees.

Questions

1. On a first deed of trust, what is the maximum interest that may be charged?

   a. No limit if the rate is stated in the loan contract
   b. 18 percent per year
   c. 20 percent per year
   d. 2 percent per month

2. What is the maximum late charge that may be assessed on a mortgage loan payment?

   a. No limit if the charge is stated in the loan contract
   b. 5 percent
   c. 10 percent
   d. 15 percent

3. Which of the following is true of VHDA loans?

   a. This program is primarily for those who already own a home.
   b. The buyer must pay all discount points.
   c. A power of attorney cannot be used to execute documents.
   d. A higher down payment is required for VHDA-VA and VHDA-FHA loans

4. When borrowers sign a note and deed of trust, what have they agreed to regarding a court hearing if they default?

   a. To request the hearing within 30 days of default notice
   b. To permit the lender to set the place and time of the hearing
   c. To waive the hearing
   d. To abide by the court's ruling without appeal

5. Which of the following statements is true regarding a loan that is sold outside Virginia?

   a. The note must be acknowledged and recorded.
   b. The note must be notarized.
   c. The deed must be notarized.
   d. A loan secured by Virginia property may not be sold out of state.

6. The responsibility for preparing any promissory notes involved in a closing belongs to the

   a. seller's broker.
   b. settlement attorney.
   c. lender.
   d. buyer.

7. *M* purchased a house with a conventional first deed of trust loan. *M*'s annual payment is $18,540, with monthly payments due on the tenth of each month. The loan has no provision for a grace period. If *M* makes a payment on June 18, can *M*'s lender legally impose a late charge?

   a. Yes, but no more than $154.50
   b. Yes, but no more than $77.25
   c. Yes, but no more than an amount equal to one month's interest.
   d. No: late fees on conventional first deeds of trust are illegal in Virginia.

8. *B* is granted a $40,000 maximum credit line deed of trust. He borrows $15,000 against it and then receives notice that a judgment for $10,000 has been docketed against him. *B* then withdraws $12,000 to pay other creditors; this amount is a new advance against his credit line deed of trust. The judgment creditor forecloses. Assuming the sale of the property brings enough money, what is the order in which the various amounts will be paid?

    a. $15,000, $10,000, $12,000
    b. $15,000, $12,000, $10,000
    c. $27,000, $10,000
    d. $10,000, $27,000

9. A deed of trust that permits the borrower to receive advances from time to time up to a maximum amount secured by real property is referred to as a/an

    a. conventional loan.
    b. escrow credit loan.
    c. mortgage loan deed of trust.
    d. credit line deed of trust.

10. A sales contract on a Virginia property is signed on Monday, May 1. Closing takes place on Friday, June 10, and the deed of trust is recorded on Tuesday, June 15. The borrower's first payment is due on August 30. When is the soonest that the broker receive his or her commission check?

    a. May 1
    b. June 10
    c. June 15
    d. August 30

LEASING REAL ESTATE IN VIRGINIA: PRINCIPLES

Leases and landlord-tenant relationships are governed by §55, Chapter 13, §55-217 et seq. of the Virginia Code.

Sale of Rental Property

When property that is currently being rented is sold, the new owner stands in the same legal relationship to the lessee as did the previous owner.

Appointment of Agent by Nonresident

A nonresident of Virginia who owns real property consisting of four or more rental units (whether residential or commercial) must appoint a Virginia resident as agent for the purpose of receiving any notices, service of process or other paper that would otherwise have been served on the owner. If an agent is not appointed, or if the one appointed cannot be found, the Secretary of the Commonwealth serves as agent. The secretary forwards any papers to be served on the owner to the owner's home address.

Termination of a Lease

Virginia law requires different notice periods depending on the length of the lease being terminated:

- *3-month* notice to terminate a year-to-year lease,

- *30-day* notice to terminate a month-to-month lease, or

- *120-day* written notice to terminate a month-to-month lease, where the termination is due to rehabilitation of the property or a change in the property's use (such as conversion to a condominium).

Tenant Holdover

A tenant who, through no fault of his or her own, is unable to vacate the premises at the end of the lease term is not legally held to another full term of the lease. Rather, the tenant is liable to the lessor only for use and occupation of the premises and for any loss or damage suffered by the lessor.

Desertion

If a tenant whose rent is in arrears deserts the premises, the landlord may post a written notice in a conspicuous location on the premises requiring the tenant to pay the rent. A month-to-month tenant has 10 days after the notice is posted; a yearly tenant has one month.

If the tenant fails to pay, the landlord may enter the premises, and the tenant's rights are ended. Nonetheless, the tenant still owes the rent up to the time of the landlord's reentry.

For residential tenants, Virginia law specifies that failure to pay defaulted rents within five days of receiving notice results in the tenant's forfeiture of the right to possession.

Destruction of Premises

In some states, if the improvements on leased land are destroyed, the lessee is still bound by the terms of the lease, and must continue paying full rent. Virginia has reversed and repealed this common-law doctrine. Tenants who are not at fault in the destruction of the improvements are entitled to a reduction in the amount of rent until the improvements are rebuilt and the tenants' previous use of the property can be restored.

A tenant's obligation to leave the property in good condition at the end of the lease terms is not an obligation that requires the tenant to rebuild in the event of destruction that was not his or her fault. Similarly, landlords are also under no positive duty to rebuild destroyed premises. Tenants are entitled to have the rent reduced in proportion to the diminished value of the leased premises. Tenants must prove that the destruction was not their fault and that the leased premises have been diminished in value to them.

Seizure of Tenant Property (Distress)

Goods belonging to a tenant may be seized for nonpayment of rent for up to five years after the rent is due, whether or not the lease has ended. The seizure is made by a sheriff or other officer, based on a warrant issued by a judge or magistrate. The warrant is based on a petition from the lessor. The lessor's petition must show: (1) the grounds for believing that the rent is due and (2) the exact amount owed. The lessor must post a bond.

A copy of the *distress warrant* (the order of seizure) is given to each defendant, along with a copy of the bond. The goods subject to seizure may include anything on the premises belonging to the tenant (including any assignees or subtenants) or goods that have been removed within the 30 days prior to seizure. If any of the goods seized are subject to a prior lien, the lessor's proceeds may be based only on the interest the tenant actually had in the personal property. Any sublessee is liable only to the extent that he or she owed money to the original tenant.

The seizure of a tenant's property arises from enforcing a landlord's lien, which is a statutory right. The landlord's lien relates back (that is, it attaches) to the beginning of the tenancy, not merely to the time the rent became delinquent.

If seizure of the tenant's property is made for rent due, and any irregularity or unlawful act is performed during the proceeding by or for the landlord, the tenant may sue to recover damages from the landlord. However, the act of distress itself is still lawful and the tenant still owes the rent, despite any improper enforcement actions.

If a tenant who has been served with a "pay or quit" notice pays the arrears before his or her case comes to trial, the tenant will hold the tenancy just as he or she did before the proceedings began, without a new lease or conveyance. This could be looked upon as a sort of "right of redemption," similar to a debtor's right to recover property prior to a foreclosure sale. However, a tenant may exercise this right only once in any 12-month period.

Rent Control

In 1950, the Virginia General Assembly declared that federal rent control is no longer necessary in the state.

RESIDENTIAL LANDLORD AND TENANT ACT

Title §55, Chapter 13.2, §55-248.2 of the Virginia Code, the Residential Landlord and Tenant Act, was established to protect the rights of landlords and tenants under rental agreements in Virginia.

Limitations

As the title implies, the act concerns itself only with residential property. Not everyone is subject to this act. It applies only to a property owner or owners who are natural persons (or their estates) who rent no more than ten single-family residences. In addition, if the property is located in any city or any jurisdiction that has either an urban county executive or county manager form of government, the total number of rental units combined, (both single-family dwellings and condominiums) cannot exceed four.

The act does not apply to the following:

- Nonresidential rentals

- Residence at an institution if incidental to detention or the provision of medical, geriatric, educational, counseling, religious or similar services

- Occupancy under a possession agreement by the purchaser of a property (i.e., an option contract)

- Occupancy by a member of an organization in a portion of a structure operated for the organization

- Occupancy in a hotel, motel or similar location for not more than a 30-day period

- Occupancy by an employee of a landlord whose right to occupancy is a requirement or benefit of employment (such as a property manager)

- Occupancy by an owner of a condominium unit or holder of a proprietary lease in a cooperative

- Occupancy in HUD-regulated housing, where regulation is inconsistent with the statute

- Occupancy by a tenant who pays no rent

All apartments, regardless of number owned and rented, are subject to the Residential Landlord and Tenant Act.

Application Fees

The landlord may charge a prospective tenant a fee at the time the tenant applies to lease a dwelling. If no rental agreement is reached between the landlord and the prospective tenant, the fee must be refunded within ten days if originally paid in cash, certified check or money order. If the application fee was paid by personal check, the landlord has 20 days in which to make the refund. The landlord may withhold $20 of the application fee to cover the cost of paperwork.

If an agreement is reached but the tenant does not occupy the dwelling, the landlord may withhold all or a portion of the fee to offset any cost incurred for preparing the dwelling for occupancy, holding an unoccupied unit, or for paperwork.

Unsigned or Undelivered Leases

If a written lease is not signed by either the lessor or the lessee, but the agreed rent is paid and accepted, the rental agreement is binding on both parties. Similarly, even if a lease is never delivered but the rent payments are accepted, the lease remains binding.

Security Deposits

The landlord may require the tenant to provide a security deposit at the time the property is leased. The security deposit is to protect the landlord against unpaid rents or damage (other than normal wear and tear) caused by the tenant during the lease period.

The security deposit may not exceed an amount equal to two months' rent. The deposit must be returned to the tenant within 30 days after the tenant vacates the property. If the landlord intends to withhold a portion of the security deposit to cover damages or losses, the tenant must be provided a written itemized list of such deductions.

The landlord is required to make a final inspection of the dwelling within 72 hours of the termination of the lease. The landlord must notify the tenant of the date and time of the inspection, and the inspection must be at a reasonable time. The tenant has the right to be present during the landlord's inspection but must advise the landlord in writing of the intent to be present.

When security deposits are held for 13 months or longer (in the case of renewed or multiyear leases), the landlord must pay interest to the tenant at the federal discount rate, in effect on January 1 of each year, from the effective date of the agreement. The interest is computed in annual increments and is not compounded.

Landlord's Obligations

Disclosure of Ownership. The landlord must disclose to the tenant the name and address of the property owner or anyone authorized to manage the property or otherwise act on behalf of the owner. The disclosure must be in writing and provided to the tenant prior to the beginning of the tenancy. If the property is sold, the tenant must be supplied with the name, address and telephone number of the purchaser. If the property is being converted to a condominium or cooperative, or if the tenant will be displaced due to the demolition or rehabilitation of the property within the next six months, the tenant is entitled to written notice of the situation.

Confidentiality. The landlord cannot release any financial information about a tenant to a third party without the tenant's written consent. The landlord is permitted to release information regarding the amount of rent paid for the tenant's unit, and the tenant's record of payment. A prospective buyer of rental property may have access to all tenant information, however, without the tenant's consent.

Maintenance. Landlords must ensure that the premises comply with building and housing codes affecting health and safety. A landlord must maintain the property in a fit and habitable condition and keep to common areas clean and safe. Electrical, plumbing, sanitary, heating, air conditioning and other facilities and appliances supplied by landlords must be kept in good and safe working order, and all necessary repairs must be made. Landlords are responsible for providing adequate trash removal service, running water and reasonable amounts of hot water (except when the hot water is supplied by the tenant or by a direct public utility connection).

If a landlord fails to maintain the property, the failure is considered to be a violation of the terms of a lease. The landlord could even be in violation of the law. A tenant whose landlord fails to properly maintain the premises must notify the landlord of the violation in writing. The landlord then has 30 days to correct the problem. Emergency situations warrant quicker action on the part of the landlord.

Tenants who choose to remain in a property even though a violation has not been corrected should continue to make rental payments within five days of the rental due date. However, the payments should be deposited with the general district court. To terminate a lease, a tenant must file a claim with the general district court.

House Rule Changes. During the period of occupancy, the landlord may adopt additional minor changes to the rules and regulations. However, changes to "house rules" may not alter the terms and conditions of the lease. For instance, a change in the hours the swimming pool is open or a requirement that parking decals must be displayed on vehicles would be appropriate house rule changes; a change in the number of persons permitted in each unit would not be an appropriate midlease change. The landlord must give reasonable written notice of any rule changes.

Rule changes that substantially alter the rental agreement are only valid if the tenant agrees in writing to the changes. The tenant may refuse to accept the changes and insist on being bound only by the conditions of the original lease. However, at the expiration of the rental agreement, the tenant must either accept the changes or vacate the property.

Right to Access. The landlord must give the tenant reasonable notice of intent to enter the property, except in the case of an emergency. The tenant cannot deny a landlord's reasonable request, provided the landlord does not abuse the right. If the landlord abuses the right of access, the tenant may seek an injunction from the circuit court.

Tenant's Obligations

In addition to the lease provisions, the tenant has additional responsibilities under the law.

Condition of Property. A tenant must keep the leased premises as clean and safe as conditions permit. Garbage must be removed regularly. The facilities and equipment (including heating, plumbing, electrical, sanitary, air conditioning and appliances) must be used in a reasonable manner. Tenants may not destroy or remove any part of the premises or permit anyone else to do so, either through negligence or deliberate act.

Behavior. Tenants must conduct themselves in a manner that will not disturb neighbors. Each tenant is expected to abide by all reasonable rules and regulations established by the landlord.

Violation of Rental Agreement. If a tenant violates the terms of a lease, the landlord must notify the tenant of the violation in writing, and allow the tenant 21 days to correct the violation. If the tenant fails to take corrective action, the lease will terminate at the end of 30 days.

If repairs, replacement or cleaning will correct the violation, the landlord may enter the property, correct the problem and charge the tenant for any costs incurred. Under normal circumstances, the landlord must give the tenant 14 days' written notice prior to entering the premises. In an emergency, however, the landlord may enter and correct the violation as promptly as necessary.

Nonpayment of Rent. If rent payments are not received when due, the landlord may take the following actions:

- *Five Day Pay-or-Quit Notice.* The landlord may issue a written notice giving the tenant five days to pay the rent or to vacate the property.

- *Unlawful Detainer Warrant.* The landlord may begin eviction proceedings immediately after issuing this warrant. The tenant remains obligated to pay rent.

- *Eviction.* If full payment of rent is not received within five days, the landlord may file suit to have the tenant evicted. The landlord may not remove or exclude the tenant from the property or deny essential services until such time as the court takes eviction action.

Returned Checks. If the tenant issues a check that is returned for insufficient funds, the landlord may give notice requiring payment in cash, cashier's check or certified check within five days. If payment is not received, the landlord may proceed as with nonpayment of rent.

Security Devices. Tenants may install security equipment at their own expense. The property must be restored to its original condition on termination of the lease. Tenants must provide the landlord complete operating instructions, along with keys, codes and passwords for any equipment installed.

Absence from the Property. If a tenant plans to be absent from the property for more than seven days, the landlord may enter the property for the purpose of protecting it. If the terms of the lease require tenant notification of extended absences, and the tenant fails to advise the landlord, the tenant may be responsible for any damage that occurs during the absence.

Automatic Renewal Clauses

Many leases contain *automatic renewal clauses*. The clause specifies that the lease will automatically renew under the same terms and conditions unless either party gives written notice within a specific number of days prior to the termination date. Any changes, such as a rent increase, must be agreed to in writing by the tenant. Failure to agree to any changes constitutes notice to vacate. In the event that all terms and conditions, including rent, remain unchanged, the renewal of a rental agreement is considered to be a new agreement.

Early Termination by Military Personnel

Military personnel who are transferred must be allowed to terminate a valid lease by giving the landlord at least 30 days' written notice and a copy of the official orders. Early termination

cannot take place more than 60 days prior to the date necessary to comply with the orders.

The landlord may charge one month's rent as damages if the tenant occupied the property for less than six months *or* half of one month's rental if the tenancy was more than six months but less than one year.

Subleases

If the lease allows a tenant to sublease, the landlord must approve or disapprove the sublessee within ten days of written notification. Failure to respond within this time constitutes approval of the sublessee.

Disposal of Abandoned Property

Personal property left on the premises after the termination of a lease may be considered abandoned. The landlord may dispose of the abandoned property as he or she sees fit or appropriate, provided ten days' written notice has been given to the tenant. Any funds received from the sale of the abandoned property may be used to offset debts owed by the tenant, including the cost of moving and storing the abandoned property. Excess funds are treated as a security deposit.

Prohibited Lease Provisions

Virginia law does not permit the following provisions in residential leases:

- An agreement to waive any rights granted by Virginia law

- A confession of judgment or *cognovit* clause — an agreement by the tenant to permit an attorney to enter a confession of judgment against him or her in the event of a lawsuit arising out of the lease)

- An agreement to pay the landlord's attorney fees (with certain exceptions)

- An agreement to limit the landlord's liability to the tenant or indemnify the landlord for the liability or any attendant costs

Any of these provisions, if included in a residential lease, is unenforceable. The inclusion of an unenforceable provision does not, however, void the lease.

Retaliatory Action

A landlord may not retaliate against a tenant who sues or otherwise seeks to enforce his or her legal rights or rights under the lease. Rent increases, a decrease in service, or termination of the lease are all barred retaliatory actions.

The tenant is protected from retaliation if the landlord has notice of any of the following:

- The tenant has complained to the government about building code violations or conditions dangerous to health or safety

- The tenant has made a complaint to or filed suit against the landlord for violation of any provision of the Residential Landlord and Tenant Act

- The tenant has organized or has become a member of a tenants' organization

- The tenant has testified against the landlord in court

- The tenant has complained about possible Fair Housing Law violations

The act does not prevent a landlord from increasing rent in order to bring the property into line with prevailing market rentals for similar property. A landlord is also free to decrease services. The changes, however, must apply equally to all tenants.

MANAGEMENT RESPONSIBILITY

A property manager shares the owner's responsibility for ensuring that landlord-tenant relations comply with the Residential Landlord and Tenant Act. As the owner's agent, a property manager could be liable for any violations, especially fair housing and tenant's rights issues.

Questions

1. *G*, who lives in Virginia, is acting as resident agent for *T*, who lives in Los Angeles. *T* owns an apartment building in Alexandria. When a tenant is injured on the premises and decides to sue *T*, *G* is on an extended vacation and cannot be located when the notices are served. Who will receive these notices?

    a. The sheriff
    b. The president of the tenants' association
    c. *T*
    d. The Secretary of the Commonwealth

2. *H* owns the Cherry Run apartment complex, which has fallen into disrepair. *H* decides to repair and renovate the buildings, and convert them to condominiums. How much notice is required to terminate the tenants' month-to-month leases?

    a. 30 days
    b. 60 days
    c. 90 days
    d. 120 days

3. Four months before her lease expires, *V* abandons her apartment, stops paying rent and disappears. *V* leaves her furniture and an expensive entertainment center behind. If the landlord sells the apartment's contents at a "garage sale," which of the following is true?

    a. *V*'s obligation to pay rent for the lease term ends if the sale nets an amount equal to the outstanding rent.
    b. Because the landlord failed to obtain a distress warrant, *V* is relieved of all obligations under the lease, and is entitled to damages.
    c. *V* may be entitled to damages for the landlord's unlawful seizure, but because the seizure was for rent due, *V* is not relieved of the obligation to pay the outstanding rent.
    d. The landlord acted improperly: no seizure of a tenant's property is lawful until the lease has ended.

4. A tenant rents farmland, a barn and a house. The buildings are destroyed by a fire caused by lightning. Must the tenant still pay rent and abide by all the terms of the lease?

    a. Yes, based on common law principles governing ground leases.
    b. Yes; any damage to or destruction of the leased premises is the tenant's responsibility.
    c. No; destruction of the improvements terminates a ground lease.
    d. No; if the tenant is not at fault, he or she is entitled to release from the lease or a reduction in rent until his or her use of the land is restored.

5. *B* entered into a one-year lease on July 1, 1999, with the right to continue on a month-to-month basis after the lease expires. *B* gave the landlord a security deposit. In accordance with the terms of the lease, *B* gives proper notice and vacates the property on October 31, 2000. How much interest will accrue on *B*'s security deposit?

   a. None
   b. 4 months
   c. 12 months
   d. 16 months

6. A one-year lease period begins on April 1, 1999. The tenant stops paying rent on July 1, the notice to quit is received on August 1, and the landlord's lien is recorded on December 15. When does the landlord's lien attach to the tenant's property?

   a. April 1, 1999
   b. July 1, 1999
   c. August 6, 1999
   d. April 1, 2000

7. A prospective tenant applies for a lease in the Seven Hills apartment building and pays the mandatory $125 application fee. If the tenant decides not to sign a lease, what happens to the application fee?

   a. The fee may be kept by Seven Hills.
   b. The fee must be returned to the prospective tenant within 20 days.
   c. The fee must be returned to the prospective tenant, less a 10 percent charge to cover paperwork.
   d. The fee must be returned to the prospective tenant, less $10 to cover the cost of paperwork.

8. A cognovit clause is:

   a. legal in residential leases only.
   b. legal in nonresidential leases.
   c. legal in all leases.
   d. illegal in all leases.

9. A landlord who is subject to the Residential Landlord and Tenant Act charges $750 per month for an apartment. What is the maximum amount the landlord can require as a security deposit?

   a. $750   c. $1,500
   b. $1,000   d. $2,250

10. During a crime wave, a tenant decides to install a burglar alarm in a rented house. Does the tenant need to inform the landlord?

   a. No; the tenant has full right of possession during the lease.
   b. No; only tenants in multi-unit apartment buildings are required to inform a landlord about a security system.
   c. Yes; the tenant must also give the landlord instructions and passwords.
   d. Yes; but the cost of the system may be deducted from the rent.

13 Fair Housing and Ethical Practices

The Virginia Fair Housing Law [Title 36, Chapter 5.1, §36.96.1] states that it is the policy of the Commonwealth to provide for fair housing throughout the Commonwealth, to all its citizens *regardless of race, color, religion, national origin, sex, elderliness, familial status, or handicap.* All discriminatory practices in residential housing transactions are prohibited.

Virginia's fair housing law has been ruled substantially equivalent to the federal fair housing law. It is an exercise of the state's police power for the protection of the peace, health, safety, prosperity and general welfare of the people of Virginia.

All *inhabitants* of Virginia are protected by the Fair Housing Law, whether or not they are also citizens of the Commonwealth.

Protected Classes

The Fair Housing Law's prohibits discrimination in housing and real estate activities on the basis of

- race
- sex
- color
- familial status
- religion
- handicap
- national origin
- elderliness

Definitions

Certain terms in the Fair Housing Law have specific legal definitions.

Dwelling. A *dwelling* refers to all or part of any building or structure designated or intended for use as a residence by one or more families. The term also includes vacant land offered for sale or lease for the construction or location of any residential building or structure.

Elderliness. For purposes of the Fair Housing Law, an "elderly" person is any individual who has attained his or her 55th birthday.

Familial status. The Fair Housing Law protects families against discrimination. A *family* is defined as a parent or other person who has legal custody of one or more individuals under the age of 18 who live with the parent or other person. The definition also extends to persons with custody of a minor with the written permission of a parent or guardian. The term also includes pregnant women and people who are in the process of securing legal custody of a minor.

Handicap. A person is considered "handicapped" if he or she suffers from a physical or mental impairment that substantially limits one or more of his or her major life activities. Having a record of such an impairment, or being regarded as having such an impairment, also constitutes handicaps under the Fair Housing Law. The statute does not apply to persons who use or are addicted to illegal substances. Transvestites are specifically excluded from the definition of handicap.

EXEMPTIONS

As with the federal law, there are some exemptions in Virginia.

- A single-family residence sold or rented by the owner is exempt from the statute, as long as the owner owns no more than three homes at the time and, in the case of a sale, has not sold more than one rental property in the past 24 months. This exemption applies only if an owner does not employ the services of a real estate licensee and no discriminatory advertising is used.

- Rooms or units in 1–4 family structures are exempt if the owner occupies one of the units and does not use discriminatory advertising.

- Religious organizations, institutions, associations or societies may limit the sale or rental of property they own or operate for other than commercial purposes to persons of the same religion. Such organizations may give preference to their members, as long as membership in the organization is not restricted on the basis of race, color, national origin, sex, elderliness, familial status or handicap.

- Private, state-owned or state-supported educational institutions, hospitals, nursing homes, religious organizations and correctional institutions may, for personal privacy reasons, require single-sex occupancy of its owned and operated single-family residences, rooms and units. Single-sex restrooms in such dwellings or buildings are not illegal.

- Private membership clubs that provide lodging that they own or operate for other than commercial purposes may give preference to their members.

Advertising for Shared Dwellings

An individual who intends to share his or her living quarters with another may advertise on the basis of sex, but only on the basis of sex. For example, an ad could say "Females only need apply," but it could not say Christian females or white females.

Single-Family Occupancy

Certain restrictive covenants and zoning laws exist that restrict housing in an area to single-family housing. According to Virginia law, a family care home, foster home or group home in which no more than eight persons reside who are mentally ill, retarded or developmentally disabled, together with resident counselors or staff, is considered single-family occupancy for zoning purposes. For purposes of restrictive covenants, there is no maximum number of residents.

A condominium unit owners' association may, if permitted by the bylaws, restrict the number of occupants in any unit, as long as the limitation is reasonable and not more restrictive than the local zoning ordinance.

Housing for Elderly Persons

It is legal to discriminate on the basis of age to permit housing for elderly persons. Housing is exempt from the familial status protection if it is provided under a state or federal program designed to assist the elderly, or is intended for and solely occupied by persons at least 62 years of age, or has at least one person 55 years of age or older in 80 percent of the occupied units. Qualified housing in this second category must provide the elderly with important housing opportunities and adhere to published policies and procedures that demonstrate the intent to provide such housing.

Criminal Background

People who have been convicted of the illegal manufacture or distribution of controlled substances are not protected by the fair housing law.

Rental applications may require the disclosure of any criminal convictions, and applicants may be required to consent to (and pay for) a criminal background check. A building manager or property owner may refuse to rent a dwelling to an individual who has a record of prior criminal convictions involving harm to persons or property, and whose presence would pose a threat to the health or safety of others.

Similarly, the law's protections do not make it unlawful for an owner to deny or limit residential rentals to persons who pose a clear and present threat of substantial harm to others or the premises.

IN PRACTICE . . .
Local counties, cities and towns may enforce legislation adopted prior to 1991 that is *more restrictive* than either the state or the federal law. Any amendments to the local legislation, however, must conform to the state's law. Because licensees often operate in more than one jurisdiction within the state, they must be aware of all local legislation that differs from federal and state laws.

Impact for Real Estate Licensees

It is illegal for real estate licensees to be involved in discriminatory housing practices in any way. While licensees should be aware of the exemptions in order to fully comply with the law, it is of more vital importance that they comply with the law's nondiscriminatory intent. §36.96.2A states that:

> this exemption shall not apply to or inure to the benefit of any licensee of the Real Estate Board, regardless of whether the licensee is acting in his personal or professional capacity.

UNLAWFUL DISCRIMINATORY HOUSING PRACTICES

In Virginia, it is illegal for anyone to commit any of the following discriminatory acts on the basis of a person's race, color, religion, national origin, sex, handicap, elderliness or familial status:

- Refusing to sell or rent a dwelling to any person who has made a bona fide offer to do so, or refusing to negotiate the sale or rental of a dwelling

- Discriminating against any person in the terms, condition or privileges of the sale or rental of a dwelling, or in providing services or facilities

- Making, printing or publishing any notice, statement or advertisement with respect to the sale or rental of a dwelling that indicates an actual or intended preference, limitation or discrimination

- Falsely representing that a dwelling is not available for inspection, sale or rental

- Denying membership or participation in a multiple listing service (MLS), real estate brokers' organization or any other service, organization or facility related to the business of selling or renting dwellings

- Including any discriminatory restrictive covenant in the transfer, sale, rental or lease of housing, or honoring any discriminatory restriction

- Inducing or attempting to induce the sale or rental of a dwelling by representations regarding the entry or prospective entry into the neighborhood of protected persons

- Refusing to sell, rent or negotiate with anyone on the basis of their own handicap, or that of anyone who will be residing in the dwelling, or anyone associated with them

- Discriminating in the terms, conditions or privileges of the sale or rental of a dwelling, or in its services or facilities on the basis of an individual's handicap, or that of anyone associated with the individual

IN PRACTICE . . .

The use of words or symbols associated with a particular religion, national origin, sex or race is considered prima facie evidence of an illegal preference. The use of such words or symbols may not be overcome by a general disclaimer that no discrimination is intended.

Special Rule Regarding Handicapped Persons

Handicapped individuals (that is, persons with disabilities), must be permitted to make reasonable modifications, at their own expense, of existing premises in order to make the premises fully accessible to the individual. A landlord may make modification of rented premises conditional on the tenant's agreement to restore the premises to its original condition (reasonable wear and tear excepted).

It is unlawful to refuse to make reasonable accommodations in rules, practices, policies or services in order to afford handicapped individuals equal opportunities to use and enjoy a dwelling. For instance, a "no pets" policy should be flexible enough to accommodate service animals, such as a seeing-eye dog or an assistance monkey.

New multifamily dwellings (that is, with four or more units) must be designed and constructed in such a way that the public use and common areas are readily accessible to handicapped persons. All ground-floor unit doors must allow passage by persons in wheelchairs, and contain light switches, electrical outlets and environmental controls that are accessible by persons in wheelchairs. Kitchens and bathrooms must be designed for full maneuverability. In buildings with elevators, all units must meet the accessibility requirements.

Lending Institutions

The Fair Housing Law also applies to lending institutions and other businesses involved in residential real estate transactions. It is unlawful to discriminate in the availability, terms or conditions of real estate financing on the basis of race, color, religion, national origin, sex, elderliness, familial status or handicap. Discrimination on the basis of financial qualification is permitted, however.

If any lending institution is found to be engaging in unlawful discriminatory practices, the Fair Housing Law forbids state, county, city or municipal treasurers or other government officials from depositing public funds in the institution. Existing deposits of public funds must be withdrawn from offending lenders, although the action may be deferred for one year to avoid financial loss to the state, county, city or agency. If the lender corrects its practices, there is no prohibition against the deposit of public funds.

The Virginia fair housing law also applies to those who are involved indirectly in the sale or rental of real property, such as newspapers and other publications. Appraisers cannot include any discriminatory information in appraisal reports.

ENFORCEMENT OF THE FAIR HOUSING LAW

Persons who feels that their rights under the fair housing law have been violated may take action against the party alleged to have discriminated. Complaints must be filed with the Real Estate Board (REB), which is empowered to initiate and receive complaints, investigate alleged violations, and resolve conflict either by conference and conciliation or by issuing a charge and referring the matter to the Attorney General for action.

A complaint must be filed with the REB within one year of the occurrence or termination of the alleged discriminatory practice.

In any action brought under the Fair Housing Act, the burden of proof is upon the complainant. The REB must acknowledge receipt of the complaint and advise the claimant of time limits and choices of forums for hearing the complaint.

Accused persons must be notified of the allegation and of their legal rights within ten days. Proceedings must commence within 30 days after receiving the complaint. The investigation must be completed within 100 days. While the investigation may take longer than 100 days in some circumstances, no investigation may take more than a year from the date of the complaint.

The REB may issue subpoenas, interview witnesses, and request the production of documents in the course of its investigation. During the investigative period, it is possible for the complainant and respondent to enter into a conciliation agreement, subject to REB approval.

If reasonable cause exists to believe that a discriminatory housing practice has occurred or is about to occur, the REB must seek resolution by conciliation or forward the charge to the attorney general for civil action. If no reasonable cause exists the case will be dismissed.

Penalties

If the case results in civil action by the Attorney General, the court may

- award preventive relief by temporary or permanent injunction, restraining order, or other necessary order;

- award other appropriate relief, including compensatory or punitive damages;

- assess civil penalties (in cases involving zoning or land use ordinances, patterns or practices of discrimination or the breach of a conciliation agreement) of up to $50,000 for a first violation and up to $100,000 for any subsequent violation; and

- award the prevailing party reasonable attorney's fees and costs.

Whether or not a complaint has been filed with the REB, a civil action may also be initiated by an injured person in a U.S. district court or state court within two years after the occurrence or termination of an alleged discriminatory housing practice. If a conciliation agreement is breached, a civil action may be filed within two years of the breach.

Actions Against Licensees

If any real estate licensee is found guilty of violating the fair housing law, the REB will take appropriate steps to consider suspension or revocation of the license, or take other disciplinary action.

Questions

1. An owner may discriminate on the basis of religion in selling or renting his or her own house in which of the following situations?

    a. The ad clearly states that religion is a criterion.
    b. The broker is fully informed of the religion criterion.
    c. The owner already owns four other properties rented to persons of the same religion.
    d. The owner is a religious organization or institution.

2. A building manager receives a lease application from T, a prospective tenant. The application discloses that T served time in prison for income tax evasion. T now has regular income from a manufacturing job and otherwise meets the building's qualification standards. Can the building manager lawfully refuse to rent an apartment to T?

    a. No; the Fair Housing Law prohibits discrimination on the basis of prior criminal record.
    b. No; T's criminal conviction did not involve harm to persons or property.
    c. Yes; the Fair Housing Law permits a building manager to refuse to rent to any convicted criminal.
    d. Yes; the Fair Housing Law does not apply to actions by building managers.

3. W, a real estate licensee, is found to have violated the Fair Housing Law. What are the REB's options regarding W?

    a. Binding arbitration only
    b. The REB must revoke W's license.
    c. The REB may suspend or revoke W's license, or take other disciplinary action.
    d. The REB may only refuse to renew W's license at the time it expires.

4. All of the following are protected by the Virginia Fair Housing Law's provisions for the handicapped or elderly EXCEPT

    a. A 55-year old recovered heroin addict.
    b. A 62-year old cocaine user.
    c. A paralyzed veteran.
    d. A mentally ill person.

5. Investigations of fair housing complaints must be completed within how long after a complaint is filed?

    a. 30 days   c. 100 days
    b. 60 days   d. 2 years

6. A civil action brought by the attorney general for a first violation of the Virginia fair housing law could subject a guilty party to a monetary civil penalty of

    a. up to $10,000 for a first offense.
    b. up to $25,000 for a first offense.
    c. up to $50,000 for a first offense
    d. actual damages and legal fees only.

7. Which of the following is protected by the Virginia Fair Housing Law?

    a. Marital status
    b. Familial status
    c. Source of income
    d. Dietary restriction

8. Mary was looking for someone to share her house. She placed the following advertisement in the local paper:

    Share lovely town house. Large wooded lot, near transp, shops and recreation. $650 per mo. Nonsmoker, female.

    Which of the following is true?

    a. The ad is a violation of the Fair Housing Law because it discriminates against people who smoke.
    b. The ad violates the Fair Housing Law's prohibition against sexual discrimination.
    c. The ad is legal because Mary is sharing her own home.
    d. The newspaper is now subject to a civil action for publishing a discriminatory ad.

9. Two people apply for a mortgage loan from Mighty Mortgage Company: *R*, a 65-year old blind male with no income or savings; and *S*, a 35-year old black female with no debts and a six-figure income from her law practice. Based on these facts alone, if both *R* and *S* are turned down, Mighty Mortgage has most likely committed unlawful discrimination against:

    a. *R* only
    b. *S* only
    c. Both *R* and *S*
    d. Neither *R* nor *S*

10. The Leefield County Board of Real Estate Licensees is a professional organization that provides local real estate professionals with listing information, marketing assistance and monthly networking luncheons. There are no other professional organizations in the county. All the board's members attend the United Central Church. A licensee who is a member of the Country Temple applies for membership on the board and is rejected. Which of the following statements is true?

    a. The rejection is legal because the board's members attend the same religious organization.
    b. The rejection is legal because it was not on the basis of the applicant's race.
    c. The rejection is illegal because nonreligious membership clubs may not discriminate against applicants.
    d. The rejection is illegal because the board is an organization related to the business of selling or renting dwellings.

Practice Examination

1. Salesperson *S* represents Seller *K* and Salesperson *B* represents Buyer *J* in the same transaction. *S* and *B* both work for Broker *N*. In this situation, *S* is known as:

   A. Associate broker
   B. Dual agent
   C. Single agent
   D. Designated agent

2. Who of the following must hold a real estate license in Virginia?

   A. An attorney preparing an abstract of title
   B. A local MLS company
   C. An officer of a limited liability company that specializes in commercial property
   D. A business executive selling her company's surplus acreage

3. The duties that an agent owes to his or her client are established by:

   A. statute.
   B. common law.
   C. the agent's broker.
   D. the agent's client.

4. All of the following are ways to terminate a brokerage relationship EXCEPT:

   A. default by either party.
   B. death of the salesperson.
   C. expiration of the agreement.
   D. mutual agreement by the parties to terminate.

5. Disclosure and disclosure forms must contain notice advising purchasers of Megan's Law. What information is disclosed with this notice?

   A. Registered violent sexual offenders
   B. Agency representation
   C. Known property defects
   D. Stigmatized property

6. If the seller gives the buyer the required disclosure/disclaimer statement three days after the contract is signed, when can the buyer terminate the contract?

   A. Within 15 days of date sent, if e-mailed
   B. Within 10 days, if hand carried
   C. Within 5 days of postmark, if mailed
   D. Under the doctrine of caveat emptor, the buyer cannot terminate the contract.

7. If a married woman with three children dies intestate, how would her property be distributed?

   A. To her husband under laws of dower and curtesy
   B. One-third to her husband, the remaining two-thirds to her children equally
   C. One-half to her husband, the other half to her children equally
   D. Two-thirds to her husband, the remaining third to her children equally

8. *J* is an unmarried homeowner of a
    $475,000 mansion. What is the total maxi-
    mum value of *J*'s homestead exemption?

    A. $4,750   C. $237,500
    B. $5,000   D. $475,000

9. *H*, *M* and *R* are joint tenants. *M* sells his
    tenancy to *T*. Which of the following is true
    of this situation?

    A. *H*, *M* and *T* are now joint tenants.
    B. *H*, *M* and *T* are now tenants in com-
       mon.
    C. *H* and *M* are tenants in common, and *T*
       and *R* are joint tenants.
    D. *H* and *M* are joint tenants with a ten-
       ancy in common with *T*.

10. *S* and *J* are tenants in common, and *J* dies
    intestate. What happens to *J*'s interest?

    A. It passes to *J*'s heirs.
    B. It passes to *S* in severalty.
    C. It passes to *J*'s heirs and *S* as a joint
       interest.
    D. It passes to *J*'s heirs and *S* as a com-
       mon interest.

11. *K* owns an individual unit in a condomin-
    ium building and wants to sell it. Which of
    the following documents does *K* need to
    show prospective buyers before *K* can sell
    the unit?

    A. A list of any past suits or judgments
       against the condominium association
    B. A copy of the balance due on *K*'s deed
       of trust loan
    C. A copy of the current bylaws and rules
       and regulations
    D. A plat map indicating the location of
       the condominium building

12. The following is what kind of legal de-
    scription?

    All those certain lots, pieces or parcels of
    land, situated in the city of Roanoke,
    Virginia, known, numbered and
    designated on the Plat of Hampton
    Square and recorded in the clerk's office
    of the Circuit Court of the City of
    Roanoke, Virginia, in Map Book 26,
    page 7, as Lots No. 9 and 10.

    A. Metes-and-bounds
    B. Rectangular survey
    C. Government survey
    D. Lot-and-block

13. What is the most common method of
    describing real estate in Virginia?

    A. Combination of metes-and-bounds and
       government survey
    B. Combination of metes-and-bounds and
       lot-and-block
    C. Combination of lot-and-block and
       government survey
    D. Combination of rectangular survey and
       government survey

14. If a contractor records a mechanic's
    memorandum of lien on September 15,
    2000, how long does he or she have to file
    a suit to enforce it?

    A. Until October 15, 2000
    B. Until December 31, 2000
    C. Until March 15, 2001
    D. Until September 15, 2001

15. If all of the following liens are recorded
    against a property and the owner fore-
    closes, which will be paid first?

    A. Real estate tax lien
    B. Mechanic's lien
    C. Deed of trust lien
    D. Vendor's lien

16. *P* owns a house in severalty and wishes to sell it. His broker tells him that his wife, *N*, will need to sign the contract even though she does not own the property. Why would this be the case?

    A. *N* is required to sign the contract under the Statute of Frauds.
    B. *N* is required to sign the contract to convert the equitable title into legal title.
    C. *N* is required to sign the contract so that the title is "marketable."
    D. *N* is required to release any future interest in the property she might hold.

17. An implied warranty against structural defects on new construction continues for how long?

    A. Six months after the date of transfer of title or the buyer's taking possession
    B. One year after the date of transfer of title or the buyer's taking possession
    C. Two years after the date of transfer of title or the buyer's taking possession
    D. Five years after the date of transfer of title or the buyer's taking possession

18. All of the following are requirements for a valid deed EXCEPT:

    A. signature of the grantee.
    B. consideration.
    C. accurate legal description of the property.
    D. delivery and acceptance of the deed.

19. *F* buys *T*'s home for $149,500. Which of the following is a correct statement of the grantor and recordation taxes to be paid?

    A. *F* will pay $224.25; *T* will pay 224.25.
    B. *F* will pay $224.25; *T* will pay $74.75.
    C. *F* will pay $299.00; *T* will pay $149.50.
    D. *F* will pay $149.50; *T* will pay $299.00.

20. The Virginia requirement that a deed of trust be recorded and all settlement proceeds be distributed within two days of the date of settlement is covered under what statute?

    A. Fair Lending Act
    B. Residential Deed of Trust Act
    C. Statute of Frauds
    D. Wet Settlement Act

21. All of the following are information found on a title report EXCEPT:

    A. easements and covenants.
    B. buyer's full legal name.
    C. status of taxes.
    D. existing lenders.

22. Which of the following is an accurate description of the Real Estate Board?

    A. Seven members; five licensees and two consumers
    B. Seven members; six licensees and one consumer
    C. Nine members; seven licensees and two consumers
    D. Nine members; either licensed brokers or salespersons

23. If a licensee is found guilty of a violation of the license law or rules and regulations, the Real Estate Board may take all of the following disciplinary actions EXCEPT:

    A. imposing a prison sentence of no more than one year.
    B. levying fines.
    C. denying license renewal.
    D. suspending or revoking a license.

24. The Real Estate Board's activities include which of the following activities?

    A. Arbitrates disputes between salespersons and brokers
    B. Issues real estate licenses
    C. Recommends commission rates and commission splits
    D. Approves standardized listing agreements and sales contracts

25. K's license is about to expire so she signs up for some continuing education classes. She takes two hours of Virginia real estate laws and regulations, two hours of ethics and standards of conduct, two hours of real estate taxes, and two hours of escrow requirements. Assuming K successfully completes these courses, will she have met her renewal education requirements?

    A. Yes, because she has completed at least eight hours of continuing education
    B. No, because she has failed to take a course on federal real estate laws
    C. No, because she has failed to take a course on the Americans with Disabilities Act
    D. No, because she has failed to take a course on fair housing laws

26. J accidentally let his salesperson's license expire, but two months later is ready to renew it. How much money does J need to send to the Real Estate Board for his renewal fee?

    A. $46.00
    B. $100.00
    C. $146.00
    D. $190.00

27. Salesperson R is getting married and will be changing her last name. What must she do to inform the Real Estate Board?

    A. Notify the REB within 30 days of the wedding
    B. Notify the REB within 45 days of the wedding
    C. Notify the REB within 60 days of the wedding
    D. Notify the REB before her license renewal deadline

28. C has a Virginia salesperson's license, but is currently holding it in inactive status. She decides to sell her home with the help of a local brokerage firm. Should she disclose her license status to potential buyers?

    A. Yes, because disclosure is required regardless of an inactive license status
    B. No, because the local brokerage firm will be earning the commission from the sale
    C. No, because disclosure is not required when a licensee sells his or her own home
    D. No, because disclosure is not required when a license is inactive

29. Salesperson *W* finds a buyer for a home he has listed. The buyer gives *W* an earnest money cashier's check for $2,000. What should *W* do with the check?

    A. Keep it until closing
    B. Deposit it in his escrow account within three business banking days
    C. Deposit it in his escrow account within five business banking days
    D. Immediately give it to his broker

30. If the Real Estate Transaction Recovery Fund falls below $400,000, how much money may the Real Estate Board assess each licensee?

    A. $20 from each salesperson; $40 from each broker
    B. $20 from each inactive licensee; $40 from each active licensee
    C. $20 from each salesperson and broker, inactive or active
    D. $40 from each salesperson and broker, inactive or active

31. All of the following actions are considered improper delivery of instruments EXCEPT:

    A. failing to promptly deliver complete and legible copies of any written contracts to each party in a transaction.
    B. using "bait and switch" tactics through advertising.
    C. failing to deliver a complete and accurate statement of money received and disbursed by a licensee.
    D. failing to provide timely, written notice of any material change in the transaction to all parties.

32. *H* completes his real estate salesperson course on June 20, 2000. He then takes and passes the Virginia licensing exam on July 15, 2000. How long does *H* have to apply for his license before being required to retake the exam?

    A. Until December 20, 2000
    B. Until January 15, 2001
    C. Until June 20, 2001
    D. Until July 15, 2001

33. Salesperson *R* decides to leave Broker *K*'s firm and work at Broker *M*'s firm. How should the Real Estate Board be notified of this change?

    A. *R* should file a "Change of Brokerage" form with the REB.
    B. *K* should give *R*'s license to *M*.
    C. *R* and *M* should apply to the REB to have a new license issued.
    D. *R* and *K* should file a "Termination of Brokerage" form with the REB.

34. Which of the following statements is true regarding institutional financing in Virginia?

    A. Mortgage loans, rather than deeds of trust, are the instruments primarily used in residential sales transactions.
    B. VA and FHA notes require notarization to be valid.
    C. Late charges on a loan may not exceed three percent of the installment due.
    D. Due-on-sale clauses are prohibited in Virginia.

35. Foreclosure of a deed of trust by decree of court is what type of foreclosure?

    A. Strict foreclosure
    B. Deed in lieu of foreclosure
    C. Trustee sale
    D. Equitable foreclosure

36. F entered into a one-year lease on October 1, 2000, with the right to continue on a month-to-month basis after the lease expires. F gave the landlord a security deposit. In accordance with the terms of the lease, F gives proper notice and vacates the property on December 31, 2001. How much interest will accrue on F's security deposit?

    A. None
    B. 2 months
    C. 12 months
    D. 14 months

37. If a tenant leaves a couch and two chairs in his apartment after the lease has ended, is the landlord allowed to sell it?

    A. Yes, provided the tenant is given ten days' written notice
    B. Yes, within one week of the lease's termination date
    C. No, Virginia includes a nonabandoned property clause in all leases
    D. No, the furniture remains the property of the tenant

38. Which of the following is protected by Virginia's Fair Housing Law?

    A. A 58-year old AIDS victim
    B. A 45-year old homosexual
    C. A 35-year old transvestite
    D. A 51-year old veteran

39. All of the following apartment building accommodations for handicapped persons are considered reasonable EXCEPT:

    A. allowing a blind person to have an assistance monkey in a "no-pets" building.
    B. allowing a paralyzed person to install railings in his or her bathroom.
    C. removing walls along a corridor of a common area to make the hallway wide enough for wheelchair access.
    D. giving first-floor unit preferences to a wheelchair-bound person.

40. If an alleged fair housing discriminatory act has taken place, how long after the occurance of the act does the injured party have to file a complaint with the Real Estate Board?

    A. Three months
    B. Six months
    C. Nine months
    D. One year

Answer Key

The correct answers to the chapter review problems appear below. Each answer is followed by a reference to the page number of the chapter on which the answer is explained.

CHAPTER 1
1. a *2*
2. c *4, 5*
3. c *3*
4. d *1*
5. d *6*

CHAPTER 2
1. b *11*
2. a *11*
3. c *13*
4. c *21*
5. d *20*

CHAPTER 3
1. c *23*
2. a *23*
3. b *23*
4. b *25*
5. a *23*
6. b *25*
7. d *26*
8. b *26*

CHAPTER 4
1. c *29*
2. a *29*
3. b *29*
4. b *29*
5. c *32*
6. d *30*
7. b *33*
8. b *31*
9. b *37*
10. a *34*
11. b *36*
12. b *35*
13. b *37*
14. d *30*

CHAPTER 5
1. d *41*
2. d *42*
3. c *42*
4. d *42*

CHAPTER 6
1. a *45*
2. b *45*
3. d *45*
4. b *46*
5. a *45*
6. b *47*
7. c *47*
8. c *48*
9. b *48*
10. d *49*

CHAPTER 7
1. d *53*
2. a *61*
3. c *61*
4. d *53*

CHAPTER 8
1. d *63*
2. b *63*
3. c *63*
4. d *63*
5. a *64*
6. b *64*
7. c *65*
8. b *66*

CHAPTER 9
1. d *69*
2. b *69, 70*
3. a *69*
4. d *69*
5. c *69*
6. d *71*
7. a *70*
8. b *70*

CHAPTER 10
1. c *78*
2. b *87*
3. b *81*
4. c *86*
5. a *79*
6. d *75*
7. a *78*
8. b *89*
9. c *81*
10. b *82*
11. d *86*
12. d *92*
13. d *81*
14. a *99*
15. c *88*
16. b *90*
17. d *96*
18. c *89*
19. c *96*
20. d *96*
21. b *95*
22. d *96*
23. c *100*
24. d *98*
25. a *94*
26. d *90-91*
27. a *88*
28. b *92*
29. d *77*
30. a *78*

CHAPTER 11
1. a *111*
2. b *108*
3. c *109*
4. c *107*
5. b *108*
6. b *107*
7. b *108*
8. a *108*
9. d *108*
10. c *112*

CHAPTER 12
1. d *115*
2. d *115*
3. c *116*
4. d *116*
5. c *118*
6. a *116*
7. d *117*
8. b *121*
9. c *118*
10. c *120*

CHAPTER 13
1. d *125*
2. b *126*
3. c *129*
4. b *124*
5. c *128*
6. c *128*
7. b *124*
8. c *125*
9. b *127*
10. d *126*

PRACTICE EXAMINATION

1.	d	*1*	11.	c	*34*	21.	b	*70*	31.	b	*97*
2.	c	*2, 76*	12.	d	*41*	22.	c	*75*	32.	d	*77*
3.	a	*3*	13.	b	*41*	23.	a	*75*	33.	c	*87*
4.	b	*5*	14.	c	*48*	24.	b	*76*	34.	b	*108*
5.	a	*20*	15.	a	*46*	25.	d	*82*	35.	a	*110*
6.	c	*13*	16.	d	*61*	26.	b	*85*	36.	c	*118*
7.	b	*24*	17.	b	*61*	27.	a	*87*	37.	a	*120*
8.	b	*25*	18.	a	*63*	28.	a	*88*	38.	a	*124*
9.	d	*29*	19.	c	*64*	29.	d	*88*	39.	c	*127*
10.	a	*29*	20.	d	*69*	30.	c	*92*	40.	d	*128*

Index